LEAP SEVEN

Launching Entrepreneurial Avenues of Possibilities

MARILYN CARROLL

DEDICATION

TO MY MOTHER,

thanks for always being there for me

TO MY KIDS,

thanks for listening and believing in me.

TO MY FRIENDS,

thanks for supporting me and believing in my vision and ideas

CONTENTS

ACKNOWLEDGMENTS

I am grateful to the many people who helped with this book helped to make the LEAP SEVEN movement. I want to first acknowledge Taylor Fraser for designing the logo and brand material for LEAP SEVEN. Robert McDowell for being there for me 100% through research and writing of the book. Shelia Hollie for heading the LEAP SEVEN t-shirts and Dallas, Texas launch of LEAP SEVEN. Jane Theobald Stein for suggesting I write the book. Charlene Benn for suggesting that we build an organization around LEAP SEVEN. Justine Duhr and her team for their help in coaching and editing. Also, Chrystal Bernard for consistently being there for me on decisions I needed to make and her help in organizing LEAP SEVEN.

INTRODUCTION

Knowledge is the product of relationships.

This book, LEAP SEVEN, is about getting what you want. It's about achieving success in the kind of work you have always wanted to do, and it's about doing so with empathy and ethical consideration for others. It's about translating your dreams into real-life experience. Yes, you can have it all, and you can have it while growing into the best version of yourself ever. You can be a success and a good person at the same time, you can perform wonderful, beneficial acts for others along the way, and you can learn how to sustain your wonderful life once you've achieved your initial goals. This is the life-transforming journey that LEAP SEVEN promises. LEAP SEVEN does not waste your time with empty promises or pie-in-the-sky scenarios. LEAP SEVEN deals in widely accepted truths and proven examples of how to build and sustain relationships, launch your own business, and understand and make use of the social networking available to the savvy entrepreneur.

As an entrepreneur, I've experienced so many highs and lows. I like to say that I, like many entrepreneurs, am and have always been (and always will be) what I call a **LEAPER**. LEAPERS go from one project to the next based on what we feel passionate about. We pay attention to the big and small picture and make efforts to engage others based on mutual needs. Yes, I have witnessed and experienced success and failure.

I was asked once what LEAP truly means to me, besides **Launching Entrepreneurial Avenues of Possibilities**. *Great question!* I thought. I considered carefully before responding, and here is the answer I came up with: I have been a leader all my life. No matter where I find myself within an organization, my family, business, or any other circumstance, I find that I am leading, that I am practicing leadership. I realized that I am often filling the role of a person of influence in any setting, no matter where or what it is. I studied leadership at the highest levels, practically and academically, and became an expert in leadership. The first letter in **LEAP** stands for my leadership component.

All through my entrepreneurial life, my ability to grasp complex situations, perceive solutions, and successfully manage people and processes has been at the heart of my success. At every step, I have been able to trust in and draw on my ability to infuse creativity and innovation into complex situations. As a result, I excel at solving challenges and transforming that which seems impossible into that which is not only possible but productive. As an entrepreneur, I found myself succeeding at this process again and again.

You can't be afraid to try something new when something old no longer works. The successful entrepreneur has to stay on the cutting edge and be willing to do the unexpected to achieve unexpected results. Believing in this as I do, throughout my life I have found myself consistently exhibiting entrepreneurial characteristics in my day-to-day work and career. Even when I was an employee rather than an employer, I drew on those characteristics to guide my performance.

For example, I recall a time when I worked as a group vice president at a bank. One day, I learned that my team's work in the 401(k) Daily Valuations Department was going to be eliminated and sent to a technology-driven outside company. This move would impact me and many others, so I saw an opportunity to come up with a plan that was needed, though not immediately clear to everybody. It was imperative that I come up with a winning strategy. My goal was to hold on to as many as possible of the talented individuals who helped make my career and the bank a success.

After studying the situation from all possible angles, I perceived that my team was very talented in compliance testing, conversions, plan document reviews, and document restatements, while the company that was slated to replace my team largely lacked these skills. My team also boasted a strong knowledge base in ERISA (Employment Retirement Income

Security Act of 1974), something that was surprisingly rare in many

institutions. I could see that if the outsourcing went on as planned, it would

create a gaping hole at the bank. Because I recognized that this hole would

develop, I was able to make a formal suggestion to the bank that we needed

to retain much of my talented team in order to launch and maintain our

own in-house compliance group. After careful review of my proposal, the

bank accepted it, creating job security and continuity for my team. The

second letter in **LEAP** represents my entrepreneurial component.

The A in **LEAP** stands for my academic component. It is no secret

that I love to learn, and have always been that way. The desire to learn is my

top strength, according to Marcus Buckingham and Donald O. Clifton's

book, *StrengthsFinder*. I am always in learning mode. I learn from situations

every day, enjoying the flow of knowledge I get from conversations, news,

books, articles, reports, retreats, workshops, students, and social media

communications. Learning gives me the freedom and resources to make

informed decisions through critical analysis of diverse, wide-ranging

information. It is through this learning that I've been able to advance my

leadership (L) and entrepreneurial (E) skills and keep them thriving,

developing them into limitless possibilities.

For example, I enjoyed the opportunity to be on a movie set for four months, where I learned firsthand about the industry. Thanks to my personal experiences and research, I developed a vision for a potential business that would fill a need I perceived in two industries. That process of evaluation, planning, and execution led to even greater opportunities in the entertainment and education industries.

This brings me to the final letter in **LEAP** and my personal association with it. The P represents the seven traits that build my brand: These traits are passion, positivity, persistence, preference, power, potential, and perseverance. Each one of these seven dynamic traits inform every move I make. When I'm exploring options or planning my next career and business moves, I rely on these traits to guide me and keep me on an appropriate path. These traits are the legs that hold me up when I am weak. They sustain me over the long haul. They are pillars and they help me maintain balance as I find and develop connections and friendships. These seven LEAP traits are also evident in the personal and professional circles that I surround myself with wherever I am. They are the wisdom and guidance that direct me. These are the seven traits that complete me as I make my way through my entrepreneurial, career, business, and personal journeys.

Are you ready to LEAP SEVEN with me? Are you ready to turn your life into the life you want? Let's go!

Imagine the grand, wide avenues of Paris, considered by many to be the most beautiful streets in the world. Now imagine that these lovely boulevards represent your dreams of becoming a self-employed entrepreneur: Watch them morph into the network of avenues that lead to the realization of your entrepreneurial life. Can you see them, full of light, stretching out to the horizon? Can you see them intersecting, curling into and out of each other, creating fascinating byways and leading to exciting destinations? Well, those avenues of possibility converge right here! They converge in your entrepreneurial self and in the social networks you establish and nurture. They are made up of the words, sentences, paragraphs, chapters, examples, and exercises found in LEAP SEVEN, and if you heed them well, you'll successfully launch your new entrepreneurial life of freedom, adventure, and financial gain. Let LEAP SEVEN guide you!

Here is a simple exercise to get you started. All of us must start this new journey from where we are right now. So, let's begin! Make a list of all the jobs you've had to this point in your life. How many jobs have you had? Don't forget those early jobs you worked as a teenager! Once you have finished your list, sit with it for a spell. Enjoy—or cringe at!—the memories that pop up in your mind. Think about the things you learned at those jobs, the people you met and how they helped or hindered you. You might even think of some people associated with certain jobs who made no impression on you at all.

The point of this exercise? Just an important realization, which is this: All the jobs you've ever had, all the work you've ever done, have combined to make you the person you are today. They have been an integral part of your education, a series of highways that have led you to this present moment. Those jobs have also affected your dreams, especially your dreams about work, what you want to do, and who you want to be.

Once you have your list, ask yourself how does it reflect your current job? If you have one, what is your current job? Are you doing today what you have always wanted to do? Are you happy in your work? Perhaps you are in transition. If you are in transition, where are you going, and how confident are you that you will actually get there? Perhaps you know what you want to do, but you haven't quite gotten to the point where you *can* do it.

Is this you? If it is, you are not alone. Millions of people experience this stage of a working life's journey. Many workers feel they are trapped by responsibilities. Some have dependents to care for or debts to pay, and some are simply paralyzed by the fear of change. So they continue on, doing work they don't care about, or even despise, while dreaming of that wonderful job that is out there, somewhere. And so a friend of mine who always wanted to be an archaeologist continues to work in the pet store he's been with for five years. And maybe there's a bartender who would love to be a stonemason, but he's developed a little drinking problem and loves the big tips. Or imagine a retail clerk who dreams of starting her own fashion design company, but has no confidence in her abilities to make it happen. People everywhere dream—big dreams and small dreams—about their true calling. They dream, and they defer, and they watch the time pass.

Time passes, but it doesn't mean that opportunity ends: Fortunately, opportunity has no time limit. There is no deadline for breaking through, for waking up one day and just knowing that everything has changed, especially you, and that the life you want to be living is really, finally beginning. It's as if everything in the world—other people, trees, plants, animals, water, roads, buildings, sky, sun, moon, stars—is saying to you, "Welcome! What took you so long?"

We are living in a terrific historic time, a LEAP SEVEN time. The world has never been more entrepreneurial and full of opportunity than it is today. It's now accepted as a universal truth that the average person will have as many as twelve careers during a long lifetime. That's a lot of careers, and a huge cultural shift from the way people lived just fifty years ago. Back then, most people learned one trade or skill, or attended college to master a profession. Many of them fully expected to remain, and succeed, in their chosen walks of life, and many did.

Then the technological revolution exploded and personal computers, social media, and social networks made the world smaller and much more intimate. Business that once took two weeks to carry out was now transacted in a matter of hours. Unlikely allies became mutually sustaining partners. People discovered, and reveled in, greater mobility. They were no longer rooted to a physical place, or to just one job. At the same time, more and more people began living the dream of working for themselves. For the first time, for many, that dream actually seemed possible.

This development was no fad, no passing fancy. There would be no going back to doing business as we used to do it. There was some nostalgia for the old ways, but most people soon adjusted as they awoke to more abundant opportunities. This trend has given rise to a golden age—a golden age of entrepreneurs and entrepreneurship.

One doesn't have to be an entrepreneur idol like Mark Zuckerberg, Sheryl Sandberg, J.K. Rowling, Elon Musk, Jeff Bezos, or Jack Ma to be an entrepreneurial success. There are limitless degrees of success, just as there are limitless opportunities for achieving it. The key is finding your sweet spot where satisfaction, performance, and results meet in flexible balance.

You will learn in LEAP SEVEN that you, like every other person you meet, work with, and serve, are unique. You will eventually see yourself not as all things to some people, but many things to many people. This is a subtle yet important distinction. The successful entrepreneur knows how to become both the water in the cup and the cup itself.

Never before has there been such a need for the LEAP SEVEN approach and a book like this one. In our bold new entrepreneurial world, an up-to-the-minute guide and roadmap can shorten the learning curve and speed up the process of achieving success.

Before I describe the seven chapters that follow this introduction, let's take a moment to consider what entrepreneurialism means and what it looks like to be an entrepreneur.

"Entrepreneur" comes from a nineteenth-century French word that literally means "director of a musical institution." In the twenty-first century, we can modify this to mean "one who directs; one who sings her or his own song." Isn't that what an entrepreneur does—sing her or his own song? That's what an entrepreneur *wants* to do. It's what a successful entrepreneur must do.

A person who wants to be an entrepreneur wants to work for herself. For many today, it is a longstanding dream. But being one's own boss, and the employer of others, brings with it many challenges and responsibilities, in addition to obvious benefits.

What are those benefits? To begin with, you get to do something you love. You set your own agenda, often even your own hours. In a collaborative spirit, you are responsible for deciding the direction your business takes. You also enjoy the challenge and process of making decisions, accepting responsibility, and being fair to others. You make every good-faith effort to take care of yourself and inspire others. You are the wind filling out the sails and guiding your ship to its perfect destination.

The challenges of entrepreneurship are real, too. It's no secret that entrepreneurs deal with more anxiety than their employees. Being an entrepreneur can be stressful! Entrepreneurs have to guard against neglecting their health. Sometimes they don't sleep enough and they forget to exercise; they don't eat enough or they eat too much or they eat badly. Some beginners are plagued by unreasonable fear of failure. Self-confidence can take a beating. Sometimes entrepreneurs must figure out how to stay in business through periods of chronic underfunding.

Yet setbacks ought to be seen as only temporary. Almost every start-up needs time to find its stride and begin to make money. The entrepreneur (and investors and employees) must exercise patience. The successful entrepreneur will also develop the ability to turn disappointment or failure into success. This is all about vision and point of view. The successful entrepreneur has the ability to absorb setbacks, and to look at them not as crippling body blows and knockout punches, but as opportunities to learn and grow. Disappointments are transformed into the building blocks of greater success. This positive outlook becomes part of every successful entrepreneur's emotional makeup, and this journey we are on together here will help you to find this strength in yourself. Think of this as the beginning of relationship building that will become a hallmark of your entire entrepreneurial LEAP SEVEN life.

The seven chapters that follow will help you to identify yourself as an entrepreneur. You will discover your value statement and your true mission, and you will clarify your goals. Insights, examples, and exercises will guide you through the process of building a knowledge value chain that is focused on relationship building. Why? *Because relationships are the true key to any successful entrepreneurial endeavor.* Without successful relationships, entrepreneurial effort never gets past the "Gee, I wish" stage. My LEAP SEVEN approach will teach you the art of building successful relationships for mutual benefit and will rocket you past the dreamer stage.

Along the way, you'll learn real skills that will help you excel in your entrepreneurial pursuits. You'll get to know yourself better and increase your social acumen, becoming more competent, comfortable, and professional in networking and in your day-to-day life. You'll learn how to engage in effective conversations and communicate your expert knowledge without bragging or showing off. You will learn how to use your sense of humor. You'll create new value and have a greater impact, increasing the contributions you make to your organization, profession, and team. More and more, you will develop relationships of mutual benefit and nurture your ever-growing circle of influence. You will learn what it means to master the universal approach, the mentoring approach, and the targeting approach while building community and business. You will also learn how to master operational, personal, and strategic social networking, as well as learning how combining these approaches can help you achieve what you are trying to accomplish.

You will also master the practical process of adopting a networking marketing mindset, because *communicating about what you do is as important as doing it*. You will discover how to plan, focus, and follow through. You will also find ways to nurture your creativity and discover how to be innovative and how to collaborate effectively with others.

Let's consider the mission, values, and goals of LEAP SEVEN itself.

LEAP SEVEN Mission:

To create a collaborative community of intentional networks invested in the professional growth of members.

LEAP SEVEN Values:

Members act as allies who are innovative and spur change for the communities in which LEAP SEVEN members live and work. Why? We believe in cohesion, and that strength in members leads to openness and sharing to create something new that complements and helps all.

LEAP SEVEN Goals:

Our goals are to facilitate growth in relationships; foster intentional network expansion; inspire collaboration with diverse professional allies who invest in each other's professional growth; challenge traditional practices and build innovative solutions for the future.

Now we're prepared to move forward, to start a new entrepreneurial life by planning for success. Are you eager to get started, to move from dreaming and wishing to doing? Well, then, turn the page and begin!

2

PLAN FOR SUCCESS

"Dreaming, after all, is a form of planning." —Gloria Steinem

Human beings are unique in many ways. We have thumbs! We also have language, the amazing gift that ensures that we can talk to one another. When language was first discovered and developed, the talking started and never stopped. Honestly, that's where business began. As soon as we could talk, it was inevitable that many of us would become entrepreneurs.

One thing humans do besides talk is plan. Human beings love to build things and to make lists, resolutions, and outlines. We think of things we would like to do and see made, and we organize our thoughts accordingly. Is this all it takes to plan for success? Does one just have a dream or a great idea, run with it, and then welcome success along the way? Well, not often, not really. If only! But we know better. Don't we all know people who plan and plan but somehow never seem to move beyond the planning stage? Of course we do. In fact, we may be, or have been, one of those people at one time or another! If we are, or were, we know how hard it is to overcome the inertia of planning or dreaming, and of wanting to simply stay at that stage forever.

We also know people who dream and desire, then jump into action without many resources or much planning. These impulsive doers fare little better than the procrastinators. There really is a difference between thinking, dreaming, planning—and *doing*. LEAP SEVEN comes after the dreaming and the wishing. LEAP SEVEN is all about planning *and* doing.

This is something I realized while working in Atlanta as the CEO of a security company, providing security to the stars on the set of a major motion picture. I found this new role amazing, and I experienced more than a few "How did I get here?" moments. I got there because of an opportunity that came to me through a friend. Even before that, it came first to my friend through another friend. Those two people had a long relationship over many years, and in their discussions they often talked about some of the challenges they were facing or had dealt with in the past. Based on one of those conversations, my friend asked for my help in putting in a bid to do some new work. That conversation led to me taking a trip from Dallas to Atlanta to complete the job of staffing, hiring, and getting a license to perform security services in the film industry in Atlanta. Beginning there, I found that my initial experience opened doors in other markets in which I and my staff performed the same services. This is how my business got started, and it all came about because of an opportunity presented to me by a close friend who connected me to *his* friend. It all began with social networking, almost before I really knew that was what I was doing!

That experience was amazing and very insightful. It allowed me to see even more business opportunities in this field and in other fields, too. For example, I reconnected with a friend who is the president of the chamber of commerce in a major city. She was so helpful, connecting me with her area's film industry contacts, which led in turn to additional film security opportunities and contacts in the industry. Gradually, I learned that for every link I might receive from a connection, there is the possibility, even the probability, of additional connections. This one connection led me to six other opportunities to expand and grow my new business. There is no way that would have happened for me without the magical opportunities that come from social networking.

Opportunities from these social and business connections come in many forms. One has to be flexible and always open to accepting the challenge of a new opportunity if one is to make the most of these connections. It is imperative that everybody involved feel proud of the fact that they opened doors to the right person. People love to feel useful, to feel as if they really helped someone else. You can't get hung up on and blocked by what you don't have, including contacts and experience you believe is valuable. In my case, the process of starting and running a company was the most important experience I could ever dream of or possibly have. The entire process more deeply awakened me to my varied skills, which include the strength and willingness to learn and persevere.

This reminds me of my first job opportunity out of college, which originated as a result of a surprising suggestion made by my accounting professor. The truth is, I hadn't even noticed that she was particularly aware of me until she approached me one day after class and shared the news that a friend of hers had a job opportunity. The job involved working in the auditing department of a CPA firm, helping to prepare returns during tax season and audits during other parts of the year. She told me that based on my work ethic in her course, she felt that I should definitely apply for the job and give it a shot. I followed her advice, and to my surprise I got the job! I was thrilled, of course, but I quickly came back to earth. I had to admit to myself that I felt out of my league. I spent weeks crying. I realized I had some serious life lessons to learn, including how to take on a challenge with no experience or training in that particular area.

You see, completing tax returns was the easy part; working with retirement plans was a different story. In college, I had learned nothing about the Employment Retirement Income Security Act of 1974, and I hadn't learned anything about the Tax Reform Act of 1986 and its impact on retirement plans. A partner of the firm decided that he needed someone to help out in his retirement group, and, with advice from my boss and based on my work during the tax season, he decided that someone would be me. I spent many, many hours in the tax and legal library of the firm poring over tax law and studying. Often, I had to give up spending as much time as I wanted to with family and friends. However, the experience helped to pave the way for me to earn the income I needed to support a healthy lifestyle for my family.

I started my first entrepreneurial adventure in college, while I was getting my master's degree. Really, before that, I had no thoughts of ever starting a business of my own. But I got a good push in school: In my capstone course we were required to start a business, and that business had to address a specific need or needs within the community. As a senior manager type, I saw firsthand that many of the students who came into my office fresh out of college for an interview lacked many of the skills necessary to fulfill the positions they hoped to land. Many of the students were high achievers academically and had attended good schools, yet they lacked many of the soft skills they would need to succeed. Based on that observation, I decided to launch a company called Up-Next Coaching for

High School and College Graduates.

The mission of this business was to work with students to help make sure they would achieve their potential after getting out of college. Because my time was limited due to other work and family, I took on only a few clients to begin with. Really, I felt that I possessed very little knowledge of how to raise the funds necessary to hire the additional resources I knew I would need in order to be successful. I had a good idea; I started well, with lots of enthusiasm and basic execution, but I suffered from bad follow-through beyond the initial execution. Why did this happen? It came down to various good reasons.

It turned out that my biggest challenge involved the advice of family and friends. Many of them were telling me that I didn't need this new business when I already had a nice-paying job and two kids to take care of. I was getting a lot of advice. I was listening, but I wasn't hearing the best advice. You see, everyone immediately around me were workers and wage earners, not entrepreneurs. They meant well, but they were *not* telling me the things I needed to hear.

Through this trial by fire, I learned something so important about myself. I learned that I truly am an entrepreneur, a manager and a businessperson with an entrepreneur's vision and involvement. You see, every job I took on my climb up the ladder toward success, and each of the roles I played, worked out in the long run because of the entrepreneurial skills I discovered, developed, polished, and exhibited. Those skills made it possible for me to carry out my multiple roles as manager, fixer, problem solver, role model, and organizational manager. Those skills developed my self-confidence, persistence, courage, and my ability to bring people together to achieve a common goal.

To be fair, let me add that I lacked the ability to connect effectively with others outside the office until later in my career. I was fine connecting with others through our kids' activities and church; I was a natural in those arenas. But I had a lot to learn about extending my social and business networks. I had to embrace the wide world. More than that, I had to learn that making outside connections beyond my immediate group was necessary if I hoped to achieve the success I so keenly desired. You see, proper and appropriate networking takes time and patience, and that's something I did not really understand when I started out. One must take the time to get to know others on several levels. It takes sensitivity, empathy, deep listening skills, and experience to learn how to help others' efforts to achieve something greater than they might be able to achieve on their own.

I want to go back for a moment to the friend who hooked me up to the film connection. He is an expert in every phase of networking. He spends hours and hours every day networking. He is constantly trying to help others, even though many of those others might think that he needs help the most. He is also generous. He is very transparent with his contacts, almost to a fault. Yet, even with all his transparency, he is sometimes misunderstood.

For eight years I have watched him make connection after connection and build a fortune in social capital in the process. Yes, he is rich in contacts, but contacts with a purpose. Over the years, he has meticulously built a fortress of contacts from every sector you can imagine of business, government, and entertainment. He has spent a lot of time doing what comes natural to him: He is a very social being. He meets many of his contacts at late-night social gatherings that take place in settings that would be seen as off-putting or even off limits to many. I look at these situations a little differently: I see them as opportunities where people are at their most vulnerable.

This issue of vulnerability should not be taken lightly or overlooked. Vulnerability opens doors. Vulnerability is actually ripe with opportunity. Contrary to some macho views, people are at their best when they are vulnerable. It's then that people are open to sharing their most intimate challenges in life and looking for non-threatening answers to the challenges they find themselves up against. My friend is always there to listen unconditionally and to help people resolve problems that they may have thought they couldn't share with others. You see, building strong networks requires deep, natural listening and patience, as well as the ability to keep secrets.

I don't mean to suggest a lot of cloak-and-dagger stuff when I write about keeping secrets. In the sharing of intimacy and information, one is always put to the test. What information should you hold close to the vest? What is appropriate for you to share with others? It is essential that a social networker never compromise shared information by speaking out of turn or by speaking in an inappropriate manner or setting. My friend has never violated this axiom, and that is largely how he has built his impressive empire of social capital.

Then there is the social capital that belongs to those in positions of power. I remember when I came up with an idea and decided that I would share it with Bill Gates of Microsoft. Of course, I didn't have his contact information, so I called a friend who had worked with him, and he provided me with an email address that would allow me to reach Mr. Gates. I outlined my idea in an email, which I sent to Mr. Gates at about 6 p.m. Central Time; the next morning I received a reply informing me that he would have someone from his office contact me. Within an hour of receiving the email I got a call from a young lady in his office who walked me through the process, providing me with directions for what I needed to do next. You see, even a relative novice, as I was at the time, can reach out to people in positions of great power and have a reasonable expectation of receiving a response and an invitation to additional engagement. These little breakthroughs require planning and patience, and, oh yes, perseverance.

Planning is bread and butter to a smart entrepreneur. The organized self-starter will always set aside an appropriate amount of time to allow for planning, but won't get stuck there. Always be planning! During the planning periods, the entrepreneur's vision of the business is allowed to take shape and ripen, to come into ever greater focus. Expectations will be refined and become more realistic. Entrepreneurs will develop greater powers of focus and perseverance. They'll begin to perceive and plan on multiple levels, and they'll begin to understand how to weather disappointment and setbacks, how to turn the unexpected or the undesired into positive outcomes and opportunities for future growth. "Make time for planning," says Stephen R. Covey. "Wars are won in the general's tent." Terence McKenna adds, "If you don't have a plan, you become part of someone else's plan." Planning lays the foundation for everything you will do in the days to come. Without it, you have no chance of success. Remember, as Gloria Steinem says, "Dreaming, after all, is a form of planning."

While planning for success, the entrepreneur is always working to identify potential customers, supporters, and markets. It's good to get into this habit right away, because it's one you will want to practice throughout your business life.

This is also the stage at which you will begin to create business plans with smart projections. There are some who argue that the traditional model of a five-year business plan is no longer necessary in our world of fast-paced business. Think again! I heartily disagree. The business plan is a living, breathing document that is your blueprint, your outline, even your lifeline to the future. It is always extremely useful, even necessary, for entrepreneurs to perform the business plan exercise of attempting to look five years into the future. Even when you complete that plan, you are not finished. Your business plan ought to be constantly revisited and updated as circumstances, changing priorities, and opportunities dictate. Why? Because like your business, your business plan is fluid and always changing. How will you know where you want to go if you don't pay attention? Entrepreneurs who embrace their business plans and really use them achieve more success than those who do not. You can look it up!

It is a fact that many entrepreneurs, after the initial dizzying excitement of starting a business, slump in their chairs, their eyes rolling back in their heads at the thought of creating the boring details of a business plan. *Oh, the humanity!* they groan. To think like this is self-defeating. It leads to brain lock and defeatism. To many entrepreneurs, a business plan is torture, a kind of punishment slapped on them by banks or boards or some other outside entity. Not surprisingly, these self-starters are heading for a fall. Few of them will ever arrive at the promised land of a business that is well established and humming along, because they balk at the essential task of formal planning—the business plan.

Others manage to see planning through a wider lens. "Good fortune is what happens when opportunity meets with planning," said Thomas Edison. Entrepreneurs who embrace Edison's words know that planning creates a positive opportunity to gather new information and learn more about themselves and their businesses. Studies have shown that entrepreneurs who are more active during the planning stage reduce the risk of later uncertainties and failures.

"Billy" was a would-be entrepreneur who couldn't wait. He hated his job in retail sales. He hated it so much that he would come in late and laze around through the day, doing just enough to get by. Of course, his lousy attitude infected everyone around him. Most of his coworkers found him irritating, even downright off-putting. Some would even tell you that they hated him. Management really started to pay attention to his issues when customers began to complain about his rudeness and poor service.

When a manager confronted him, Billy responded with belligerence, blaming others for his performance. Not surprisingly, after three such encounters, Billy was invited to find another job.

That night, alone in his apartment, Billy panicked. At first, he'd felt great about his new freedom. Then reality set in. How would he support himself? He had enough saved up to float for three months, at best, if he cut back on food and fun. Then what? Billy suffered that night, and for several days and nights afterward. Hitting bottom, he realized that maybe things really had played out as they were meant to. Maybe losing his job wasn't a disaster after all. Maybe getting fired was actually his big break!

Billy always saw himself more as a leader than a follower, and he'd always had a dream of starting and running his own business. His passion? Gaming. He thought he would be great at running a company that counseled gamers, helping obsessive gamers regain balance in their lives while still indulging their love of games. Billy decided to discuss his plans with the few family members and close friends who were still speaking to him. In general, they reacted with lukewarm to positive support, though everyone advised him to be patient, too. "Do your research, Billy," they told him, "and raise start-up capital." Someone suggested that he put together an online funding campaign. A couple of people really close to Billy even gave him personal advice about his attitude. They encouraged

Billy to examine the reasons he'd been fired. They encouraged him to sit down with a counselor about his resentment and anger issues. Most of the advice Billy received was sound, but unfortunately, Billy was a selective listener. Billy was also in a hurry.

Billy was always in a hurry. Being in a hurry, being impatient, and being a poor listener are major character flaws in any aspiring entrepreneur. Despite all the good advice he received, Billy basically heard only what he wanted to hear. Does that sound familiar? He missed a very important point, and didn't realize that the most painful things one hears are often the most important things, the things one *needs* to hear. This is usually the information that leads to growth and positive change.

Billy had a good idea, yes. That, he reasoned, was all he needed to know. So why not take the leap! Impatient, with an overinflated sense of his ability and with little planning, Billy hung out his internet shingle, advertising his company in so many slipshod and slapdash ways that an impartial observer would have lost count. Billy decided that he would pass on crafting a mission statement and a vision statement. He had even less time to spend on creating a multiyear plan. Why bother? He knew very well what he wanted to do and what he wanted out of it all. To save money, he convinced himself that he really didn't need a staff (this is a fatal flaw of people who don't work well with others yet persist in trying to get a business up and running); Billy reasoned that he could add workers as the company grew. But there was only one big problem with that idea: The company did not grow. The company teetered and swayed like the chaotic thing it was. Billy managed to attract a few customers, but they quickly soured on the "service" that Billy provided. Why? Because the service was so poorly planned and carried out. Also, Billy's poor customer relations skills had surely followed him from his old job right into his new one at his own company. Billy had managed to raise some start-up funds, mostly from family and a couple of close friends, but he swiftly burned through it all on computer upgrades, online advertising, and his own personal expenses.

In short, Billy's entrepreneurial adventure was a total disaster. Within six months, he was hanging out at the employment office and pounding the pavement looking for a job, any job, to make ends meet. For a couple of especially awful weeks, he was up before dawn to stand in the parking lot of a local paint store hoping that a contractor would hire him for the day. Billy's confidence, or should we call it his delusion, was shattered. And what was his first long-term post-entrepreneurial position? One day he found himself wearing an ill-fitting blue vest as he welcomed incoming customers at a major retail outlet and checked receipts as they left.

Of course, I retell Billy's nightmarish story here as a cautionary tale.

Let's be clear, though: The warning is not in the dream itself. Billy's dream to run his own business was a good dream. But as we look at Billy's experience, we recognize textbook examples of things that entrepreneurs should never do. Foremost among them is acting impatiently at every step. Billy may have had a good idea, but he couldn't wait long enough to perform due diligence. He ignored good advice, choosing instead to hear only what he wanted to hear. He neglected to plan—because who has time to plan, right? Really, Billy managed to do just about every wrong thing an entrepreneur can do in the start-up stage. He launched his enterprise without a real plan and with too little capital. He literally launched his business with no resources other than his eager ambition and a little money. Billy didn't just screw up. He spectacularly imploded! If only Billy had been able to slow down and plan, and develop a social network that he could turn to for help, advice, and collaboration, his experience might have been so different.

So, your first goal here ought to be that you make a promise to yourself: Promise yourself (and everyone who cares about you) that you will never turn into Billy! Entrepreneurs who plan well are much more attractive to potential funders, collaborators, and customers. They are also more savvy competitors and are more fluent with new technologies. They are even quick to grasp the complexities of regulations and efficiently and creatively comply with them. Finally, entrepreneurs in the planning stage embrace opportunities for teaming up. Many will tell you that entrepreneurs who are part of larger teams realize more success. It's true. Pooled knowledge and experience ought not to be discounted or overlooked.

For some, planning is an afterthought. For most of these people, success will prove to be elusive. Remember Billy. Don't be a Billy!

Vision Statement

As you build your vision statement, you should focus on where you are going and what you hope to achieve. Let's look at some examples of excellent vision statements:

"Build the best product, cause no unnecessary harm, use business to inspire and implement solutions to the environmental crisis." –Patagonia

"A world without Alzheimer's disease." –Alzheimer's Association

"Our vision is to create a better every-day life for many people." – IKEA

"To become the world's most loved, most flown, and most profitable airline." –Southwest Air

"Bring inspiration and innovation to every athlete* in the world. (*If you have a body, you are an athlete.)" –Nike

"To be the best quick service restaurant experience. Being the best means providing outstanding quality, service, cleanliness, and value, so that we make every customer in every restaurant smile." –McDonald's

"To spread the power of optimism." –Life is good

"To inspire healthier communities by connecting people to real food." –sweetgreen

"Question Assumptions. Think Deeply. Iterate as a Lifestyle. Details, Details. Design is Everywhere. Integrity." –InVisionApp

Values inspire loyalty among employees, partners, customers, and investors. A vision statement has to inspire people. It has to have the power of motivation behind it and within it. A good vision statement has legs when it focuses on the present and the future. Anyone who reads it should instantly grasp the big picture *and* what the company will look like down the road. Readers of your vision statement should also see what makes the company different and understand why that difference matters. A vision statement must also spur on members of the organization to set and achieve highest standards.

Vision Statement Exercise

As you prepare to write your vision statement, open a Word document on your computer, or sit with a pen or pencil, and a pad of paper. Imagine having a conversation with yourself about your business. Make a list of the values you want your company to embody and represent. Make another list of the societal contributions you want your company to make. Make a third list of contributions you want your business to make to its employees. Next, make another list of the things you do *not* want your company to represent. Finally, make a list of powerful words that keep popping up in your mind as you think about your organization and its work. These words should be emotional triggers for you. (Look back at the vision statements above and pick out the words that are emotional triggers for their authors.)

After you have done this exercise to your satisfaction, share your results with close allies. Can they add anything? What do they have to say? What do they see that you do not? Consider their opinions and insights and incorporate what is valuable in them into your own vision. Now you are ready to write your vision statement. You don't have to get it right the first time. Revision for any writer is a blessing and an opportunity to get better.

Keep working on it and the right words will come and fall into place.

Mission Statement

Your mission statement is essential to the planning and the marketing of you and your business. Your mission statement should focus on the outcomes you want to achieve in your professional and personal life. The mission statement says what a company's mission is and why. The mission statement states what you do and why you do it. As we did with vision statements, let's look at some examples:

"We seek to be earth's most customer-centric company for four primary customer sets: consumers, sellers, enterprises, and content creators." –Amazon

"To make people's lives better every day—naturally." –Burt's Bees

"To refresh the world; to inspire moments of optimism and happiness; to create value and make a difference." –Coca-Cola

"To inspire and nurture the human spirit—one person, one cup and one neighborhood at a time." –Starbucks

"To bring inspiration and innovation to every athlete in the world." – Nike

"[To make] the world a more caring place by helping people laugh, love, heal, say thanks, reach out and make meaningful connections with others." –Hallmark

"To give people the power to share and make the world more open and connected." –Facebook

"To give everyone the power to create and share ideas and information instantly, without barriers." –Twitter

"Spread ideas." –TED

As you can see, the mission statement can be made up of many or very few words. In TED's case, it's all of two words! Just as clear should be the realization that the mission statement is not the same thing as the vision statement. The vision statement is a big-picture view of your organization; the mission statement answers questions beginning with whom, how, and what: Whom are you in business to serve? How will you do what you want to do? What *do* you do, and what is valuable about it? No mission statement succeeds if it does not answer these questions in concise, declarative language.

Mission Statement Checklist

When writing your mission statement, keep the following suggestions in mind:

Begin your mission statement with an action verb.

Make sure your goal is large.

Embrace brevity and be memorable.

Use plain language—no fifty-cent words!

Avoid using words like "assist," "facilitate," or "help."

Focus on a specific problem that needs fixing.

Mission Statement Exercise

Make a list of the kinds of people you hope to serve in your business. What is their age range and gender? What is their level of education? Where do they live? What do they do?

Next, make a list of the ways you intend to reach and serve these people. For instance, will you send them a newsletter every two weeks? Every month? Will you offer a special membership of some kind? What will you do to make them feel special and essential to you?

Then make a list of the things you do and what is special about them.

Finally, share summaries of your lists with stakeholders and potential stakeholders (even potential customers). Consider their insights and opinions and incorporate what is valuable into your sense of your mission. When you have done all this work, you are ready to write your mission statement.

Like your vision statement, you should regard your mission statement as a living, breathing organism, an essential part of the body of your organization or business. Periodically, you'll revise and update your mission statement. Do so gladly. Seek and embrace input from employees, investors, networkers, distributors, and customers. Revising your mission statement is an important opportunity to expand and develop your community based on collaborative partnerships. As the map of what, for whom, and how you will do what you do, your mission statement is an essential guide and companion on the road to success.

As we plan for success, with vision statement and mission statement in hand, we want to envision and plan for our ideal network, identify potential contacts, and capitalize on opportunities for both. To maximize our results, we can use three different approaches: universal, mentoring, and targeted.

Universal Approach

Many theories describe variations of the universal approach to planning. All of them seek to quantify the current value of a customer and that customer's potential value. In other words, what makes this person so great, and what can she or he do for us? The frequency of a customer's "participation" or "engagement" with your company is pretty straightforward; predicting that customer's future intent is more mysterious and difficult. What is it that you will have to do to ensure that this customer remains committed to you and your company over the long haul?

Customers can be notoriously fickle. Even the most supposedly loyal customer can turn against a company on a dime. A customer's sudden indifference is just as disheartening and potentially damaging. Losing good customers, like losing important investors, can let the air out of the office. Yet it's essential that one make a concerted effort to understand the shifting sands of her or his customer base. The universal approach provides a framework for grouping customers that encourages relevant long-range planning.

Mentoring Approach

The mentoring approach in planning calls for the recruitment and involvement of a guide (mentor) or guides during the planning process.

The word "mentor" comes from the Greek of Homer, author of *The Iliad* and *The Odyssey*. Mentor was actually a character, an older man who became the teacher and guardian of Telemachus, son of Odysseus (Ulysses). Mentor essentially raised Telemachus while his father was away from home. Odysseus was gone a long time! He spent ten years fighting in the Trojan War. Then it took him ten more years to make his way home, as he suffered a series of memorable misadventures that almost killed him. All the while, a group of men camped out at his home in an effort to convince his wife, Penelope, to marry one of them. Wealth and influence would come with such a marriage, so Penelope was a desirable potential wife. She thwarted them, however, putting them off time and again, and she protected her son as he grew to young manhood under the tutelage and additional protection of Mentor.

Ever since, mentors have figured prominently and essentially in universal rites of passage from childhood to adulthood, from nonbeliever to believer, from amateur to professional. In business planning, the mentor can oversee a planning committee's efforts by drawing on and referring to a history of successful planning that the mentor has either participated in or observed. Mentors are learned and wise. A good mentor is an effective mediator; she is someone who is adept at reconciling disagreements, however heated and contentious, and arriving at a consensus. A good mentor thrives in a creative environment and provides you with a chair and with an ear. You should feel comfortable sharing any thought or fear with your mentor because she has heard and experienced everything before. Even after the planning stage, a mentor can be a great asset to a company. No matter what comes up, you can discuss it with a mentor. Mentors pay it forward. If you survive long enough in business, it often comes to pass that you assume the position of mentor for younger entrepreneurs.

Mentor Approach Exercise

Create a list of the virtues you would like in a mentor. For instance, you will probably include empathy, deep listening, and community building. What else would be useful to you in a mentor? A sense of humor? The ability to introduce you to potential investors? Provide an entrée to an untapped customer segment?

Now, who among your acquaintances might fill the role of a successful mentor for you and your business? You may include names collected from others, too, including investors and customers. Information is power and a key to success. Also, information is never finite. It is always expanding. Information is limitless.

My Personal Mentor Story

I had an idea for a rewards program at SunTrust Bank and I contacted the CEO, Bill Rogers, to discuss it. Through an assistant, he said that he would have someone from his office contact me. Within an hour of receiving his email, a woman in his office gave me instructions to submit my idea for vetting by a SunTrust marketing team. The team came back with an unfavorable response, but in doing so it provided me with possible solutions for fixing my idea.

Not long after this, I was waiting at the Hilton in Dallas for a friend to fly in. As I waited, I met a man who was also waiting for someone. We began to talk about business, and I told him about my idea for the bank. The talk went so well that we exchanged email addresses and our intentions to keep in touch. It turned out that he owned an investment company specializing in mortgages. Through our many subsequent conversations, he shared his experiences as an entrepreneur, including all that it took him to become successful. I shared my own stories about my adventures as an entrepreneur.

For many years now, I have stayed in touch with this man, and we meet in person whenever he is in the Dallas area. I regularly seek his advice and wisdom. His advice is so important to me! He's always insightful, and he has pointed me in the direction of paths that have proven to be profitable from both economic capital and social standpoints. For example, he showed me how to approach VISA and its committee, and how to prepare myself for my presentation. He showed me what needed proof and what stood on its own based on the vision, mission, and business strategy I would present.

Most importantly, perhaps, he helped me to understand that *I* was the brand and not the product of the brand. He also helped me to realize that I am a visionary person, that I could be a great help to others as they strive to conceptualize their vision and turn it into actual products and services. He really helped me to see that I was uniquely qualified to help others put their puzzles together. This talent is one thing, but I know that without the social capital of my close friend and mentor of the last eight years, it would have been much less likely that I would have succeeded as a high-level entrepreneur. I have also learned that with every new venture or business beginning, I have needed the help of others. I have needed their advice, experience, know-how, support, and, on occasion, funding.

Targeted Approach

The targeted approach in planning identifies the needs of customers and employees, and also identifies the programs and schedules that might meet those needs. For example, planning a successful community center using the targeted approach would involve class training (visiting existing centers, organizing and conducting awareness workshops, computer training, adult education). It would involve career training, work retention training, and assessment of space and equipment needs. Planning would also have to include internet access and training, senior services, transportation, and childcare.

But that's not all. Planning would involve discovering and working outlets for creativity, and exposure to and training in multimedia publishing (personal websites, neighborhood bulletins) and computer games. Planning might also include training in how to create one's own business and providing assistance for business launches.

The targeted approach is a very specific, hands-on planning strategy that is group specific in ways that the universal and mentor approaches are not. The targeted approach assumes knowledge of potential markets, knowledge that will ensure the effectiveness of ongoing planning efforts. This is an approach that embraces diversity and adjusts with great fluency to different goals and markets. Word-of-mouth information works well in the targeted approach to planning. Throughout the process, planning should embrace the concept of helping the potential customer move from interest to purchase.

All of these strategies are effective when appropriately formed to serve the needs of the organization itself, its investors, customers, employees, and distributors. Yet, how does that happen in the most beneficial way? By focusing on potential customers and their needs. Too often, entrepreneurs in planning make the mistake of pushing plans toward where they think they should go rather than envisioning potential customers, asking what they want and how best to deliver it to them.

Whatever approach the entrepreneur chooses for planning, the proof of its success will lie in its ability to motivate people. If the plan fails to energize staff and other stakeholders, there is little hope of success at any level.

A wonderful example of success in this regard can be found at a major toy company. Because of slumping sales, a new executive team leader was appointed to a key product development group. She inherited a rather demoralized team. Sales were down, and team members were wondering how long before they lost their jobs. Their new leader correctly assessed the mood of her new team. She had extensive conversations with each team member privately, conducted exhaustive group meetings, and put all of this information together before drawing up her plan to take some bold, innovative steps.

The new manager decided that her team members needed to have more fun. She realized that they were in the business of creating cool toys. If they wanted to do it well, they needed to think more like children.

That was the key to designing and marketing cool toys that kids would actually want to play with. So, what did she do? To begin with, she renovated their workspace, making the rooms smaller (kid-sized) and painting the walls and ceilings bright colors. Lots of work was done on the floor. Team members were encouraged to draw, finger-paint, sing, sculpt with clay, and play together with toy prototypes. How would you like to show up every morning to work at a job like that?

Within three quarters, the team's morale was soaring. Sales expanded wildly, and the production team became a legend within the international company. In fact, other production departments in locations around the world adopted the team leader's ideas and realized similar results in employee and customer satisfaction, product development, and sales.

At the same time that this major toy company was experiencing a terrific boom in product development and sales, a large retail chain continued to struggle. Sales dropped so much that rescue planning seemed to change on a daily basis. Staff reductions (a generic name for layoffs and terminations) became regular events, and no one felt safe. Morale dipped to an all-time low; no one felt good. Many stores nationwide began to shut down. How could this happen?

It happened in large part because the managers and executives engaged in the planning, and in revising that planning, lost sight of their customers. Little by little, the company paid less and less attention to what its customers wanted and how the company could supply it. Planners also lost sight of the need to change, to admit that what had been so successful through the 1990s was no longer working in the second decade of the twenty-first century. When planners deny the need to change, the company will begin to wobble, and before long will be on life support.

Obviously, every entrepreneur would prefer for his or her business the successes of the toy company rather than the failures of the retail chain. Good planning involves people you know, and touches many people you may never actually meet. Trust the process.

Good planning will deliver you to the destination you desire… and so will the LEAP SEVEN approach. It can and *will* help you get there.

3

PROFESSIONAL ROI IN NETWORKING

"There is no better return on one's action than the return on the unexpected from helping others."

I cannot overstress this: Networking is all about building and nurturing relationships.

You might even say that business itself is the sum of relationships. In business, one key goal is to build communities that profitably intersect, benefiting everyone involved. These communities can intersect in many different places and on many different levels. Intersection can and often does take place both in and out of the workplace, with clients, stakeholders, and staff.

Most of us have experienced, or have observed, businesses within which various departments seem to mesh well with each other. In environments like these, workers seem to be happier and more content, for the most part, with their relationships and their work.

In other businesses, though, departments seem to exist almost as independent islands. Workers appear to be under more pressure; they do not trust colleagues in other departments and they are reluctant to cooperate or collaborate. In some very toxic cases, employees in one department may even try to subvert and damage the efforts of other departments. As models of business, which of these examples would you bet on as being more likely to succeed at all levels?

When everyone is doing well, when everyone is winning, when staffers and managers are collaborating and cooperating, doesn't the world seem like a much better and more satisfying place? Could it be that we really want to see others do well, that we want to do anything we possibly can to help others do well? Relationships are the beating heart of business. Success is impossible without successful relationships that are nurtured by participants who really do care for each other. That's the foundation we must lay before we build.

At the same time, one needs to keep an eye on the prize that is ROI—return on investment. Even this begins with healthy relationships; yet now we are going to look beyond that to examine approaches that help us understand ROI, cultivate it, and plan for it.

There is no sustainable ROI unless personal and professional objectives are aligned through a strategic approach. This alignment can appear elusive at times, because not everyone involved in networking is always on the same page. For example, you may want to tailor a network campaign to customers fitting the following description: female, age twenty to forty. But maybe your chief network guru feels a disconnect from this group. She argues for a primary campaign that targets middle-aged women *and* men, with at least high school educations and making between $30,000 and $75,000 a year. Or you may disagree over the appropriateness of a proposed program or product for school-aged children.

It's all too easy to slip into a mindset in which you're saying to yourself, "What does she or he know?" And the same thing is probably being said about you. Many businesses sag as a result of just this kind of disagreement, which, if left unresolved, turns into a series of debilitating disconnects and energy spent on futile pursuits. Not only will results suffer, but so will the potential customers and the internal morale of staff and management. It's been said many times that the public will never love a company until its employees love it first. It's so true!

ROI does not lie. Many internal planning and networking disputes can be positively resolved via a strategic approach. Accurate alignment is critical to success. If personal objectives and professional objectives conflict, it means that someone is not paying enough attention or listening closely enough to the statistics of ROI.

Then again, interpreting ROI simply as cash profit can miss the point. It's well-known in business that there is no one way to measure the success of ROI.

Why is that, you ask? Consider this example: If you invest $1,000 in a social media campaign and make $2,000 as a result, then your profit, your ROI, is $1,000. But suppose you also grow your database by five thousand names. Isn't that also a significant return on investment? Can you assign a hard number to represent that value? The answer, of course, is that you can't. There is no way to predict how many of those new names on the database will actually become paying customers or investors, or predict how much money they may bring in to the business. Just the same, all five thousand of them become stakeholders in your social media community, and you must account in some way for their presence and their impact on your company's efforts.

Really, this is your goal when you plan and seek to deepen and expand your brand awareness. Because success depends on attracting more and more satisfied customers, you measure audience reach and engagement rather than profit. In that light, those five thousand new names become significant. Not only do they swell the ranks of your customer base, a certain percentage of them will attract even more new customers. Even without a dollar sign attached to them, these five thousand new names become very important.

In considering your social media ROI, you need to think about cost and gain ratios, and that includes many factors. In your studies and reports, you must factor in training, labor, development (agencies, consultants), social media technology, a social media advertising budget, and a portion of business overhead. Potential gains that you will want to (and need to) document include page views, email signups, newsletter subscriptions, coupon redemptions, and Facebook likes, shares, and downloads.

Entrepreneurs can use metrics to demonstrate objectives achieved through social media. It's terrific to set goals and implement programs, but you're not done until you can prove the value of your efforts. Many business studies indicate that social media spending is increasing at an incredible rate. Proof of the efficacy of this spending has lagged far behind the actual numbers, but the situation is rapidly improving. Entrepreneurs in marketing are catching up. The analytical documentation they are creating will satisfy many customers and stakeholders, convincing them that you are practicing due diligence and that your claims and projections are realistic. Specific, measurable outcomes are desirable, and they're essential for building trust, shepherding your customer relations, and growing wisely.

It is important to create social capital; it is the basis for innovation and collaboration. The right collection of relationships can have a profound impact on the creation and achievement of goals, and these relationships can play a key role in marketing, and in launching products and services. Careers, even.

But let's not get ahead of ourselves. It's so important to remember that networking is about building relationships—it's not just about making a sale. Sales come later, after you have done the groundwork of building your community. The relationship is always what matters most. It's important that *you* understand who people are and that they understand who *you* are. Only then can you begin to understand what they want and what you can do for them.

As recently as three years ago (2015), studies showed that 60 percent of company employees did not understand their company's vision, mission, or values. Sixty percent! That's an amazingly terrible number! No wonder so many companies struggle. What this statistic tells us is that company leaders are not successfully communicating with their own employees, and that employees are not communicating with one another.

There are many potential reasons for this lack of communication. Perhaps some employees are not properly vetted at the interview stage; others are mismanaged or asked to perform tasks they are not up to. Managers may be neglecting employees and not following up on employee needs, suggestions, or complaints. Directives from on high may be poorly written and communicated. Really, an endless list of things can contribute to a lack of communication, which can create a toxic environment, situations like the one the statistic above describes.

Three steps can and should be taken by company leaders to address problems in communication, and all three steps can also be applied to social networking. First, employees should receive regular, consistent feedback. Second, jobs and tasks should be assigned and allocated properly. Third, everyone in a company should be appropriately recognized. Management must believe in and understand the concept that employees are stakeholders in the company, too. Without them, there really is no company. Employees must be made to feel that they are important, that they are integral members of the team. Such engagement promotes fellow feeling, which builds and nurtures community.

In similar ways, networking done well will reflect a healthy relationship with ROI. You must tailor networking efforts to specific customer segments and specific investor segments in order to achieve maximum success. For example, will a specific customer segment be more influenced by a newsletter or by a series of targeted phone calls? Answering such questions correctly, and dozens like them, will save your business time and money. With investors, you must consider what you want them to invest in, specifically, and why. It's up to you, as the business leader, and your advisors, to decide which aspect of your business is a fit for each investor. This is a fact often overlooked by leaders who are happy just to get some initial investment capital—investments that often turn into one-time events.

Social media has shrunk the world. Less than thirty years ago, few imagined that people around the entire globe would become much more intimate than ever before. Today, what once took weeks or months in business can literally be transacted in a day. It's both exciting and rather scary, the speed with which we do business! But it is *the* way now, and there is no going back to any of the older models.

Social media is critical in a business's effort to create brand awareness. Brand awareness through social media can be measured by likes, shares, or retweets, but even more information is necessary. Setting social media objectives can complement existing company and departmental goals. You might base these objectives on business conversions, customer experience, brand awareness, brand perception, and security and risk mitigation. These objectives represent what social media will help your business to achieve.

Because business moves so swiftly, it is important to establish clear-cut, easily communicated goals. It's an unwise driver who takes off on a cross-country road trip without consulting maps and picking out at least some refueling stops and overnight accommodations along the way. Your goals represent how and when you are going to arrive at your business destination. These goals need to be measurable, specific, attainable, relevant, and timely. If your objective is business conversions, for example, a good goal would be to work toward a specific number of leads you want driven by social media for the quarter. Another example of a business conversion goal would be increasing landing page conversion by 10 percent. You would measure this by tracking the conversion rate of people who land on the page through social channels.

No matter what your goals may be, audit your existing social media performance to establish baseline targets, and then set appropriate goals for improvement. The evaluation methods you use (yes, it's advisable to use multiple methods for greatest accuracy) should clearly reveal the ways in which social media helps to achieve objectives. The metrics of evaluation you use might include the following: site traffic, audience engagement, sign-ups and conversions, leads generated, and revenue generated. Whatever measurement metrics you choose, they should be able to answer these three key questions: Do they align with my objectives? Do we possess the capacity to measure effectively? Do they assist us in making the decisions we need to make and getting to where we want to go?

Measuring social media ROI is an important step in planning, one that shouldn't be underestimated, but it is not the last step. Next, you will need to select and master the proper tools to track consumers, analyze data, and accurately report the results. Here are some of the tools that are helping many businesses thrive.

Facebook is a platform that thousands of businesses rely on every day. Facebook pixels are pieces of code you can place on your website to allow you to track conversions from Facebook ads. The plugin covers both leads and sales, and can be used with various social ad targeting and optimization tools or with Facebook's own ad platform.

Hootsuite Impact is one of the social ad targeting and optimization tools widely available to entrepreneurs. Hootsuite Impact measures the ROI of social media spread across paid, owned, and earned social channels. How does Hootsuite Impact work? It connects to the analytic systems you already have in place and allows you to integrate social data with the rest of your business metrics. With the aid of Hootsuite Impact, generating executive plans and reports is a breeze. Hootsuite Impact's language is straightforward and really does a lot to optimize your social media planning and strategy.

Google is a name that should be familiar to everybody, and Google Analytics should be equally familiar. Google Analytics tracks the website traffic, sign-ups, and on-site conversions that begin with social media campaigns.

By now, you've set your goals and picked the social media analytic tools you will need. This is the point at which you actually begin to track your social media ROI. If you are properly set up, your tracking abilities will be incorporated into everything you try on social media. Because of this ability to be farsighted, you won't ever be caught short, struggling to explain and prove a campaign's success. In this fast-paced world, social media is just about the best friend that business has ever had.

An important part of successful planning is the capacity to produce useful, accurate reports, and the internet age has greatly simplified and sped up tasks that used to plague businesspeople. Today, you should be comfortable choosing and using templates that track desired metrics and present their findings in a way that is user-friendly to others. The key here is "user-friendly." Many people in business just love receiving reports. They love studying them and learning from them. Good reports to businesspeople are like comfort foods: One doesn't want to be overwhelmed with too much, but just enough is wonderful.

It should be obvious, though, and never forgotten, that although you may have made *yourself* fluent in social data speak, not everyone else has that fluency—or at least not everyone is as fluent as you may be. When you share information, you must be as clear as possible. Train yourself to use plain language! Unnecessary big words do not impress, they annoy. The last thing you want to do is turn decipherable insights into mysterious puzzles. Everyone inside and outside of your business should be able to understand and make sense of your insights and data.

The next step is often overlooked—at everyone's peril!—in a fast-paced business environment. Can you guess what it is? That's right! Don't forget to check your social media metrics *every day*. As you know, a social media campaign's lifespan is usually short; you must remain familiar with the data as it occurs and changes, as it most certainly will.

You also need to establish a timeframe that works for you, and you must stick to it. Don't veer off course if you can help it! People will come to rely on the regularity of your reports, and they will be confused and upset if you begin to miss these expected deadlines. *Don't miss them.* And if you do? Contact those who were expecting to hear from you and let them know why you missed your deadline. Ask their forgiveness and tell them when they can expect the information. This doesn't have to be like going to confession, but you need to be concise and clear. If you are, you will find that the vast majority of people are extremely forgiving. After all, who doesn't miss a deadline now and then?

So, what happens if you must report to a board or to executive directors (assuming that the board and directors are not you!) about social media ROI? No need to panic. There are wise practices for this, too.

It's important to perceive the concerns and objectives of the people you're reporting to and address them straight on. If you have done your work creating relationships and following through on them, you should have no trouble with this. Your report might say something to the effect of, "I know you want to increase teddy bear sales by 10 percent," then demonstrate how social media can contribute to that. You might do this by showing how many new sign-ups came in due to the direct email campaign targeting subscribers of the Children's Network. If teddy bear sales have not yet hit the mark, you may want to suggest tweaking the campaign to boost sales and get over the finish line.

You should also be honest about any limitations you face. You should not mislead people, intentionally or otherwise, about the information you can provide. Share the information that is demonstrable, and also make it clear that there may be some things that can't be covered by the metrics. This will save you from winding up in that awful position where you're expected to perform the impossible. That is a bad, bad place to be.

Of course, you should know that it is always a winning idea to refer to data from publications and other research firms. These can support your ideas or encourage you to change course in positive ways. The findings and opinions of other technology vendors can also be very comforting and persuasive for your stakeholders. Naturally, you may be inclined to present third-party findings that will support your own established insights and rationale. This will make your recommendations that much stronger and more likely to be accepted and supported. Sometimes, though, it's all right, and can even be wise, to share information that may appear to disagree with yours or even contradict your opinions. This can lead to a valuable discussion in which your position is strengthened by comparison, or your view is somewhat changed because you learned something you didn't know before. This truth bears repeating: *Don't fear being flexible.* Successful entrepreneurs possess the gift of flexibility. Social entrepreneurs are both the cup and the water inside the cup.

Finally, it is always a good idea to come into planning and reporting meetings with a good case for a new program or investment. You might want more money to spend on a social ad campaign, or you may want to invest in a new service or platform. But remember this: The lower the risk of this new program or investment, the better. It's smart to pluck the low-hanging fruit before reaching higher.

Once everything is up and running, it's important to remember that you have not engaged in a one-time exercise. Planning and tracking social media ROI is ongoing. And don't forget the reason why: Tracking social media ROI is about increasing long-term value while also confirming the immediate value of campaigns.

You will, of course, want to revisit the goals of specific campaigns on a regular basis. Where you find failure, don't wait: Change the campaign. Improve it as quickly as you can. To be successful, you must always update and adapt your strategy. Remember that social media and business are *never* static. This is a common truth. Be committed to change. Never hesitate or be afraid of change. Change is life itself, in business as in everything else. Take into account the changes that occur in technology and especially in customers and other stakeholders. Re-examine business priorities and key performance indicators. As an entrepreneur, you are always evolving—and so should your planning. Professionally tracking social network ROI is essential to a dynamic, successful entrepreneurial business. The size of your business doesn't matter nearly as much as your planning and flexibility. If you are successful in these realms, your business will be as big as it needs to be.

This leads me to a connection I had with a woman from the Women of Tocqueville organization. We spent a year together sharing responsibilities as volunteers and contributors to United Way. Sandy had been an ER nurse and the head of a nursing staff for over twenty-five years, and she was more or less forced into retirement as a result of downsizing.

But Sandy decided that she was too young to retire and started looking for something else to do. At the same time, her network of friends and former colleagues began calling her for help. A shortage of nurses had developed in the Dallas-Fort Worth area, so Sandy decided to start an employment service to help fill the void.

We spent an afternoon talking about the ups and downs she experienced in her start-up phase. We also talked about her success, which she attributed mostly to the relationships she had formed when she was still working as a nurse. She shared that her associates liked the way she solved problems, and that she was a great resource for others. These abilities had become so well-known that Sandy had already built a community of relationships that knew all about her abilities and her skills in selecting talent—before she even started her business. It was those skills and that community that made it possible for her to launch a successful business. She was aware of the fact that her social capital had morphed into economic capital. Today, Sandy runs her business with her daughter, whose skill sets in connecting and marketing have helped the company continue to grow. Mother and daughter combine their skills to fill a need in an underserved market. And that is exactly what entrepreneurship is all about.

4

PERSISTENCE IN FOLLOW-THROUGH

"Success occurs in there is repeated practice in perfecting one's skills and abilities."

"I get by with a little help from my friends" signifies much more than a great song by the Beatles. It suggests—no, promises—that people close to you will always be there for you. These people are so important in business. The two-way street of being there for others and others being there for you greatly enhances the possibility of success and the general quality of life you are striving to achieve, not only for yourself, but for others, too. The good intentions and energy of others complement and feed *your* good intentions and energy, encouraging follow-through and persistence.

Persistence is both an overused and a forgotten word. Everyone claims to know what it means and likes to think that he or she is persistent, yet many take persistence for granted. Many have only a hazy understanding of the word's deep meaning.

As an entrepreneur, one cannot be successful unless one is

persistent, and so it is always a good idea to find the word and the concept it represents in the words of widely admired individuals. Here are some quotes about persistence that have inspired people all over the world and, I hope, will inspire you, too.

"Energy and persistence conquer all things." –Benjamin Franklin

"Patience, persistence and perspiration make an unbeatable combination for success." –Napoleon Hill

"You may encounter many defeats, but you must not be defeated. In fact, it may be necessary to encounter the defeats, so you can know who you are, what you can rise from, how you can still come out of it." –Maya Angelou

"Ambition is the path to success. Persistence is the vehicle you arrive in." –Bill Bradley

"Paralyze resistance with persistence." –Woody Hayes

"Champions keep playing until they get it right." –Billie Jean King

"If you're going through Hell, keep going." –Winston Churchill

"If you can't fly, then run, if you can't run then walk, if you can't walk then crawl, but whatever you do you have to keep moving forward." – Martin Luther King Jr.

"Things turn out best for the people who make the best of the way things turn out." –John Wooden

Do you recognize a pattern in these famous words? Each of these individuals, and many (famous and not so famous) like them, have discovered that success lies less in genius than in persistence. Think of it as showing up, showing up every single day, no matter how you feel. If you don't show up, you can't do anything. There's a reason that *presence* and *persistence* begin with the same letter and sound and feel so similar.

In his famous book *Outliers*, Malcolm Gladwell writes that "10,000 hours is the magic number of greatness." Gladwell uses examples like the years the Beatles spent in Hamburg, Germany, playing ten hours a day, every day, honing their skills as musicians, writers, and performers before bursting onto the world's stage. The group's success was often described as meteoric, an overnight sensation. In reality, it was the product of endless grueling hours of practice, practice, practice.

Professional baseball players provide another great example of the fruits of endless preparation. When you watch a major league game, the players make fielding the ball look so easy! Nothing could be less true. What they're doing on the field is incredibly difficult, as anyone who has ever tried to play the game knows. That they usually make it look so easy is a testament to their preparation.

Gladwell meant just this: that it takes at least ten thousand hours to master a skill, any skill, be it juggling, playing the piano, building a tower out of stone, computer programming, baking, dancing ballet, or any other endeavor. He also said, "Practice isn't the thing you do once you're good. It's the thing you do that makes you good."

Persistence in practice is one of the primary habits of successful entrepreneurs. Nobody follows a quitter. A good leader must be skilled in deep listening, in organizing and planning, in persistence and follow-through.

I knew someone who ran his own start-up—right into the ground. He made many mistakes on his way to oblivion, and a big one was the way in which he treated stakeholders. He talked a great game while courting investors, and investors indeed came on board. But once he had their money in the bank, he more or less forgot about them. He justified his neglect by saying he was too busy running operations day to day. Of course, that went over like a lead balloon, as far as his investors were concerned. Not surprisingly, when in need he went to the well again, but soon he was pulling up one empty bucket after another. Investors fled.

This failing entrepreneur had violated the rule of persistence in follow-through. You can't tell an investor she is like family to you, and say that her investment in you will enrich her life in so many ways, then not speak to her again until you need more money. In what universe did he think that would work?

Another entrepreneur gradually lost the support, even the hearts, of his employees because he did not follow through on simple promises. He hinted at large raises and more paid time off in exchange for them working longer hours during a particular crisis. Trouble was, after that crisis came another, then another. It got to the point where working long hours became the standard. There were no raises and no paid time off. Even worse, the employer stopped communicating about the situation with his staff, and even seemed to get to the point where he considered their extra efforts commonplace—the new norm. Bleary-eyed staffers noted all of this over their morning coffee. There were unhappy discussions in the break room. It didn't take long for people to begin to quit. Soon there was a shortage of staff, which made the organization's problems even worse. Within eighteen months, the company closed its doors. The entrepreneur had abandoned persistence and follow-through in dealing with his staff, and, in practically no time at all, the staff abandoned him.

Yet another entrepreneur presided over a highly successful start-up.

Business was consistently good. In fact, business was better than the entrepreneur had imagined or adequately planned for.

This development can be as bad for a business as a lack of customer interest. This company took pride in its customer relations and social network specials. But as sales increased and the social network specials also grew, things began to spiral out of control. Gradually at first, then rapidly, responsiveness to customers suffered. With increasing frequency, the terms of the social network specials weren't met by the company. It wasn't long before customers took their business elsewhere. It would take a monumental effort to lure even a percentage of them back. Entrepreneurs sacrifice persistent follow-through with customers at their peril.

Lack of persistent follow-through in planning and reporting is equally destructive. You need to apply persistence to planning because planning goes on for as long as you are in business. Not long ago, research suggested that only 3 percent to 5 percent of people in business actually followed through on a consistent basis. Just by following through regularly, you will stand out as an entrepreneur.

Just be sure not to overreach. Say what you mean, and back up what you say with performance. Entrepreneurs put themselves in hot water all the time by making grand promises and then being unable or unwilling to follow through. What do customers and shareholders think of them then? Not much! They tend to fall away from businesspeople who don't back up their talk with persistent performance. They learn to distrust the big-talking, small-acting entrepreneur and look elsewhere for their business match.

You can avoid this situation by remembering some simple things. Persistently follow up with customers, distributors, and stakeholders, the kinds of people who often fail to return phone calls and emails. Work hard to connect with people you have identified as good matches, and stay connected with them over time. Don't be a fair-weather business buddy! When you do establish contact, have a plan or project ready to discuss with them. This will suggest that you are dynamic and progressive. If they put you off, ask if you can get back to them in a couple of weeks or a month. If they agree, be sure that you follow up at the designated time.

It can't be said too often that if you tell someone who is already a customer that you will do something for her, make sure you do it. This builds trust. Keeping your word will make you stand out, not only in the customer's mind, but in the business world in general. Your reputation always precedes you, so put in the effort to become known as a straight shooter who is always tactfully persistent.

Being persistent does not mean being bullheaded. You will

encounter difficulties from time to time. A staff member's performance will be disappointing; your energy will sag; you'll suddenly lose customers for no apparent reason; trusted stakeholders will leave for any number of reasons (often their own reasons that have little to do with you and your business).

When these things happen, it will be your passion for your purpose that will save you. It is persistent application of purpose that will guide you through difficulties and help you constantly discover new opportunities. Not all opportunities are the right ones, but if you persistently press on, you will find the right ones. Work and mingle with other persistent people: In business, especially, you reflect your peers, so choose them wisely.

Along the way, be persistent about celebrating your success. When you close a deal or sign a new partner or release a new social network project, take a little time to celebrate the occasion. Too often, entrepreneurs forget to smile, laugh, and have a good time. Your body needs to be fed in part on laughter and happiness, and so does your business.

Persistence Exercise #1:

I once knew an author of romance novels who, when she got great news or felt terrific about her writing, would pause and write herself a letter. Not a letter to herself on that day: a letter to herself to be read on some future day. And when that day would come, when the sky was dark, the room cold, the bills piling up, sales slacking, and not a word of good news in the morning emails, when by noon the right words would not come and her head ached, she would pull that letter from her desk drawer, tear open the envelope, and read it. And what do you suppose would happen? Think back on the John Wooden quote from earlier: "Things turn out best for the people who make the best of the way things turn out." She would read the letter and smile. She would chuckle.

None of the things that had darkened her mood would have changed; *she* changed, merely by reading her own words.

The next time you are having a really great day, take a few minutes to write yourself a letter describing why you are feeling so fine. Be sure to include lots of detail—the more the merrier. Your future glum self will thank you for it!

Persistence Exercise #2

This exercise involves keeping a list, a list that is ongoing and changeable. Begin on a day when you're in a reflective mood. Ask yourself this simple question: *What do I want to be remembered for?* That's it. Ask yourself this question, then jot down what comes to your mind and heart.

There is no right or wrong answer. Like most people, you will, over the course of time and reflection, probably think of a lot of things for which you would like to be remembered. All of them should be included on your posterity list. Some of the things you write down will be replaced along the way by other things that seem more important. That's normal.

You should revisit your list every now and then. I'm not suggesting that you need to check it every other day, but it will improve your outlook (and therefore your work performance) to refer to it perhaps a couple of times a month. Like the letter to your future self, your posterity list will make you feel better about yourself and refocus you on becoming your best self. And when those really tough, awful days hit, it's an especially good time to visit your posterity list.

The goal is to keep working, keep moving. Stay open to opportunity and don't allow setbacks or dark days to claim larger portions of your reality than they should. Bad news will come and go. The successful entrepreneur remains open to opportunity and maintains a healthy balance. The successful entrepreneur follows through.

How well would a baseball hitter do if he or she did not follow through on a swing of the bat? Think of what would happen to a performance if dancers suddenly stopped mid-turn instead of following through. The result would be arresting and awful. Following through means that you have enough self-confidence to trust the process. Following through means that you have overcome your fears, whatever they may be.

It will help if you develop habits and systems that encourage following through in every area of your life, especially in business. Many writers, for instance, create a system to help them (and motivate them to) send out their work to editors and publishers. The system is pretty simple, usually consisting of a list of places work has been sent to, the date that the work was sent, and places to send work in the future. There is also a date representing when you expect to hear back from the editor or publisher. If that date passes, you may wait another week, then contact the editor or publisher with a gentle reminder. In doing so, you must be persistent but not pushy! You simply have to communicate by *feel*. Trust your instincts and move forward. As with so many other areas of business, following through with your habits and systems is a matter of practice and more practice. The more you work your systems and good habits, the more comfortable you'll feel with them. Remember: Every interaction is a learning experience. No matter what happens, you can always change course. And often, you will find that changing course is exactly what you need to do.

As an entrepreneur, draw on your experiences of being on the job market, desperate to find work. Yes, just about everyone has been through that on many occasions. Do you remember how you went about it? For instance, did you apply for jobs simply by turning in applications and then waiting by the phone for someone to call? You probably waited a long, long time. This passive method of applying for a job rarely leads to work. What if after a week or so you had begun to look into the company for a possible personal contact? There might be one! If you had contacted such a person, she or he might have had some excellent advice to help you catch the attention of the boss or interviewer. This is an active approach. This is a good example of following through on your job application.

Or was there a time when you applied for a job, got an interview, and was told that you might be called back for a second interview? How did you handle that? Did you decide to sit back and wait for the next call (the passive approach), or did you use the time to research two other companies and apply to both of them while you waited? This is the persistent approach. This is learning the habit of following through.

Did you use social networks in your job search? A lot of people find jobs by using LinkedIn, an alumni directory, Reddit, Facebook, or some other platform. Did you find good contacts and their phone numbers, and did you have the courage to place calls to them? If you did, once again you were being persistent and following through as you should have. This persistence, this following through, in your own early job searches is essentially the same process you need to follow as a successful

entrepreneur.

This is a good point at which to recall our entrepreneurial focus on

relationships, because relationships require persistence and follow-through,

too. In business, as in life, we are the sum of our contacts. It's not enough

simply to make contact; one must follow up with and cultivate contacts.

Cultivation of contacts will lead to an increase in collaborative

opportunities, stakeholders, and revenue. Increased revenue may not

materialize as quickly as you would like it to, but it will come if you are

patient and persistent.

It is so difficult to combine these two attributes! At least, it appears

that way at first. Taking care of yourself physically helps. Think of it as

cultivating your primary relationship—the relationship with yourself. A

meditation practice will benefit you in every way. It will calm you down and

work wonders with your effort to achieve balance. Meditation is terrific for

helping you to keep things in perspective. It also rewards calm persistence.

In fact, a meditation practice instills a greater degree of balance in your day-

to-day life and work. Now, you don't have to become a Buddhist to

meditate. Jesus meditated! You don't have to assume the lotus position and

stay perfectly still for an hour to meditate. It's OK to sit comfortably in your favorite chair, keeping your eyes open or closed. It's even OK to lie down, if health issues make it difficult for you to sit. How long should you meditate? It depends. Many people derive noticeable benefits from just five minutes. Some meditate once or twice a day for ten to twenty minutes. There is no right time or method. Let your thoughts race without attempting to control them and then watch them slow down. As your racing mind slows down, you slow down. Then your mind becomes open to new insights, new visions, which you can take with you back into the workday world. You can even get results from meditating while walking! A walking meditation combines movement in nature with all the contemplative benefits. It's a lovely way to exercise your body and your consciousness. A meditation practice is a boon to your immune system, to your overall health. Its benefits will also show up in your business. I guarantee it.

Your relationship with yourself is so important! The old adage "You are what you eat (and drink)" is true, especially in this age of responsibility and risk. Entrepreneurs must guard against burnout, and watching what you eat and drink is a great place to start. In a country like the United States where obesity is rampant, train yourself to eat less and eat smaller portions. If you eat meat, that's fine, but do so in moderation. Eat a diet rich in dark-green, leafy vegetables, fruit, and omega-3s. Your immune system will thank you! Also, drink lots of water, eight to ten glasses every day. I'm guessing you already know that sodas, sugars, and processed foods are ticking time bombs that will sap your entrepreneurial energy and compromise both your performance and your health. You must eat wisely and well to succeed. You might even consider cultivating relationships with some successful chefs and restaurant owners. These are good friends to have!

In addition to a healthy diet, entrepreneurs also need to get quality sleep. This doesn't mean lying in bed grinding your teeth and worrying about the budget. It means seven to eight hours of unencumbered, restful sleep. Stress-free sleep extends life and restores the body with healing energy. Successful entrepreneurs know that there is nothing better than waking up feeling refreshed and ready to leap into the day with an attitude that embraces the inevitable challenges and knows everything will work out just as it's supposed to.

Cooperation and collaboration naturally inspire persistence. It's wise to be close to at least a few people, people who will nudge you to be persistent, to follow through, but also will let you know if you're coming on too strong. For example, you might be giving in to the tendency to call too often. Someone close to you and the situation or negotiation might suggest that email could be more appropriate of a method of following through.

Why? Because the printed word allows for space to breathe. The printed word allows for, even encourages, slower consideration than the instant back-and-forth of conversation. A close collaborator can make that suggestion to you in a way that will allow you to hear it. That kind of feedback and support is priceless and will advance your efforts.

The engineer and inventor Charles Kettering said, "It is the follow through that makes the great difference between ultimate success and failure, because it is so easy to stop." Every entrepreneur will experience moments when quitting seems like the wisest option. Usually, it isn't. Break down the wall standing in your way! Business executive Stedman Graham said, "I've found that often, just when you think you've hit the wall, you experience a breakthrough that takes you to new heights of accomplishment." Then there is this lovely Japanese proverb: "Fall seven times, stand up eight." And the amazing inventor and businessman Thomas Edison reminds us that "our greatest weakness lies in giving up. The most certain way to succeed is always to try just one more time." All you need to do is stand up one more time than you have fallen down. To stay in the game is the secret of the game itself.

5

POTENTIAL IN BENEFICIAL RELATIONSHIPS

"Ineffective people live day after day with unused potential." –

Stephen R. Covey, *The 7 Habits of Highly Effective People: Powerful Lessons in*

Personal Change

The late Fred Rogers was an expert in exploring potential in

beneficial relationships. Consider this quote from his book, *The World*

According to Mister Rogers: Important Things to Remember. "Part of the problem

with the word 'disabilities' is that it immediately suggests an inability to see

or hear or walk or do other things that many of us take for granted. But

what of people who can't feel? Or talk about their feelings? Or manage

their feelings in constructive ways? What of people who aren't able to form

close and strong relationships? And people who cannot find fulfillment in

their lives, or those who have lost hope, who live in disappointment and

bitterness and find in life no joy, no love? These, it seems to me, are the real

disabilities."

As he almost always did, Rogers saw through to the heart of the matter. He saw that an inability to form beneficial relationships is a true disability that damages not just one life, but all lives that come into contact with such negative energy. In business, this disability isn't just a deal breaker, it's a company killer.

The word "potential" implies gain and the word "beneficial" suggests positivity. Applying both words to relationships says that good things will and are happening.

For most people, the first primary relationship that holds the promise of potential and positive benefits is that between an infant and its mother. From that fundamental foundation, family relationships begin to create the landscape that will become a person's relationship map for life.

Humans are inherently social creatures. Without good relationships, life is empty. Depression and mental illness are often a result of a lack of beneficial relationships. The relationship maps of people with addiction problems and antisocial behavior are often threadbare. The absence of healthy relationships during childhood can lead to poor relationships in adulthood.

Yet many emerge from dysfunctional families and go on to create lives rich in beneficial relationships. This fact points to the compelling nature of positive relationships, to our lifelong desire to commune and work with allies. Most humans prefer relationships to a solo journey, and they work very hard to cultivate relationships that sustain them.

"Work" is an important word in that line. All beneficial relationships require diligent work. Relationships never thrive in an atmosphere of selfishness or neglect. I'm sure you can think of many examples from your own life. Perhaps you have avoided potentially beneficial relationships because you were insecure, uncertain, afraid. You may have observed others, even some people you really cared about, who seemed to sabotage themselves by undermining relationships that should have brought them rewards and joy. It's always frustrating to see relationships go south, leaving people unhappy and unfulfilled. Everyone needs community, and so the loner will never reap the benefits of the joiner.

It is much the same in business. For a business to succeed, it must be built on potential beneficial relationships.

In a healthy business, all relationships are promising. The most successful executives and managers will be attuned to this truth from the start, remaining open and fluid as a relationship begins and nurturing it at every opportunity. They won't allow a preconceived attitude or premature judgment to get in the way of genuine in-the-moment interaction. They know that judging someone can get in the way of seeing the true potential of that person. How many times have potentially good relationships been spoiled because a manager unfairly judged a newer staff member?

I knew an extraordinary high school teacher who accepted a new post in a conservative community. His credentials were impeccable. Easygoing and personable, he got along well with his new colleagues and quickly became a favorite of students. But the principal was not a fan. He bullied the new teacher from day one. He was petty and vindictive and did nothing to welcome or support the new teacher. Instead of nurturing a positive work environment, the principal poisoned the well, and soon the teacher left the school. Students wanted him back, colleagues wanted him back, but the damage was irreparable. Later, a union representative explained to the teacher that the principal had a history of targeting a new teacher every year. Who knows what motivated the principal to act like that? All that's certain is this: The principal put his own ego above the needs of the general learning community. He satisfied himself, but he damaged the students and other teachers in that community by depriving them of the promise and benefits the new teacher had brought to the school. The toll of such a loss of a relationship is immeasurable, and it's unfortunately true that such loss takes place every day; but not all the time, and not everywhere.

I'm one of those who doesn't think there is much difference

between an atomic scientist and a man who cleans the crappers

except for the luck of the draw—

parents with enough money to point you toward a more

generous death.

of course, some come through brilliantly, but

there are thousands, millions of others, bottled up, kept

from even the most minute chance to realize their potential.

—Charles Bukowski

In many businesses, sensitivity training nurtures environments of

tolerance and equanimity. Curiosity is welcomed, even rewarded. Staff and

managers are encouraged, in a safe environment, to express and explore

their feelings and attitudes. They're encouraged to share and understand

multicultural experiences and embrace gender enlightenment. These

sessions and workshops are fertile grounds for recognizing and exploring

the rich potential of relationships in the company. Unlike the toxic high

school environment in the story above, businesses with these types of

environments thrive and crackle with promise. Workers are happier and

more positive when dialogue is encouraged and differences are celebrated.

In successful businesses, the talking and sharing never stop. This isn't to suggest that business should be some kind of lovefest. Far from it! Honest exchanges can be heated sometimes. Disagreements are inevitable, no less so than in the strongest, healthiest relationships. But as we've seen before, it's all in the framing. Disagreement within a positive environment will be seen as an opportunity to learn, to expand one's horizons. Successful collaboration comes as much from healthy disagreement as from two like minds coming together.

An essential thread running through all business efforts is communication. It's not just a matter of speaking, of holding conversations in chat rooms or around a water cooler. It's not even just a matter of one person talking with another. Communication opens the door to collaboration. For instance, salespeople need to talk to marketing people, but they speak different languages. Two salespeople talking together could not welcome a marketer to the conversation and keep talking the same way. Think of it this way: As a child, you probably talked one way to your friends, another way to your parents. To communicate well and collaborate successfully, marketers and salespeople need to find a common language.

Marketing teams open doors and sales teams close them. Salespeople strive to close the deals that the marketing team creates. If these goals can be envisioned and described in ways that foster teamwork, it's a win-win situation. But at many companies, mutually beneficial relationships between sales and marketing prove to be frustratingly elusive. The more sales and marketing square off, the more tension there is throughout the company. Companies that manage to collaborate well are more resilient, more productive, more profitable.

Another example of dynamic relationships in business involves a company's developing relationships with strategic suppliers. The set-up costs for many contracts can be heavy and getting the deals done can take a long time. As the process unfolds, uncertainty and tension can erode positive energy. But deepening the relationships between parties often goes a long way toward reducing unnecessary costs, poor performance, and the need for renegotiated contracts.

Long-lasting relationships between suppliers and businesses enhance the understanding that each side has for the other's business. Suppliers gain a better and better grasp of the business's customers, its business procedures, and its markets. That the company management and staff know the suppliers so well means that there will be fewer surprises having to do with supply. More and more areas of uncertainty will dry up and disappear, and when issues do arise, both sides are positioned to handle them. The result? Improved performance.

Improved performance often involves consolidating the supply chain. With longer, deeper relationships between businesses and suppliers, buyers can make better sense of the suppliers' products and services. At the same time, suppliers will better understand the needs of its buyers. Given this bedrock of mutual support, both can confidently look for consolidation in services and products, and together identify potential new products and services. Successful consolidation allows buyers to cut their supplier stats in favor of a more streamlined and efficient supply chain.

Trust between business and supplier can allow organizations to outsource activities deemed not absolutely essential. This development usually increases efficiency and reduces internal workloads. Such trusting relationships also encourage improvements in services and products.

Potential in beneficial relationships is all talk. Literally. Not everyone you meet as an entrepreneur will prove to be an ideal or nearly ideal partner, but it would be wise to invest the substantial time and energy it takes to cultivate and follow through on every relationship. Keep in mind that as you talk, others are almost certainly talking about you. Macquarie Bank's series of legal best practice benchmark reports reveal that new business opportunities are most fertile when they come from referrals and word-of-mouth. No person and no conversation are insignificant or irrelevant.

Successful entrepreneurs know that cultivated, nurtured relationships deliver value to their businesses. That's why business plans ought to make room for the potential of beneficial relationships.

These relationships can spring from any of the following:

- Existing clients.
- Advisors to clients (financial advisors, bankers, lawyers, insurance brokers, researchers).
- Other providers (this could be any group or anyone in your field—industry associates).
- Networking groups that are appropriate to the work you do and the services you provide.

Entrepreneurs know why they cultivate and follow through on potential beneficial relationships, but again, just how does one go about it? Are there any secret formulas, an equation one can use to get there? No, but there are concrete steps that any savvy entrepreneur can take.

One step is to make sure there is cultural alignment throughout the organization. Everyone who works at the company is a spokesperson for the business and the brand or brands. The focus of your relationship partners should be in line with your own focus.

Another step involves conversation itself. Build confidence and trust by striving to find common ground. Asking open-ended questions and practicing deep listening will enrich the relationship. Find out what is important to the person you are talking to. What do they care about? Do they have something resembling a plan? Do you? Share some information with them, news you think will interest them. This can include asking straight up if there is anything you might do to help *their* business to thrive and grow. You might discover some potential for teaming up in some interesting ways.

Yet another step involves knowing when to ask for a referral. This can be tricky! If you ask at the wrong time, you may never be able to recover in that particular relationship. You have to trust your instinct and act on it. When you truly feel the time is right, act on that feeling. Ask! Ask in a straightforward, crystal-clear way. You will greatly increase the likelihood that your request will be granted if you have already done something for the person you are asking. This is just good business sense. It is also wise to ask in person. Nothing beats direct contact. It's better than asking via social media.

It takes time to develop relationships that are mutually beneficial, and that time requires patience. It also requires careful record keeping. Who at your company is responsible for which referrals? A good entrepreneur and manager will always know the answer to this question. When someone does get a referral, that prospect should be contacted within twenty-four hours. Also, the person who gave the referral ought to be thanked promptly, regardless of the outcome. After this, the process of post-referral follow-through kicks in. Your company should have a game plan, an agreed-upon policy that governs post-referral follow-through. How soon should the successful referral be contacted? How often? Once a month? Once every two months? So many businesses make the mistake of thinking that a single meeting over coffee is enough to maintain a working relationship. In most cases, it isn't. People never like to feel as if they have been taken advantage of. So many potential long-term referrals and stakeholders are lost this way! Hold internal meetings where you discuss this matter. Share information about referrals. Always remember that the goal is to establish *mutually* beneficial relationships.

"Always dream and shoot higher than you know you can do," wrote William Faulkner, Pulitzer Prize winner and Nobel laureate. "Do not bother just to be better than your contemporaries or predecessors. Try to be better than yourself." This constant striving, this holding oneself to the highest standard, is something the successful entrepreneur is always practicing. This practice makes one ready for the all-important first meeting with a referral, a potential client, investor, or stakeholder.

Ideally, this first meeting, which of course is all-important, just as every first meeting is important, should happen at your place of business.

Why? Because this is the first opportunity the visitor has of "feeling" your business, of sizing up your organization and beginning to determine if there is a good fit. The word "chemistry" is often bandied about in internal meetings, as in "Do we have chemistry with this client?" Chemistry is important, yes. But another way of thinking about the question is this: "Do we have a cultural affinity with the person?"

What does *that* mean? Well, your business's culture is defined as the reason you exist. Success with potential customers, investors, and stakeholders depends on how well you describe that and how well you can connect it to those things that are important to the individual. It's part of your pitch.

Exercise: Identifying Your Business Culture

Make a list of awards your company has received.

Make a list of all of the reasons why your employees love to come to work every day.

Make a list of testimonials from customers, investors, and stakeholders.

Make a list of what makes you different from other businesses.

During your pitch, it is useful to remember that potential customers, investors, and stakeholders enjoy camaraderie, but they want even more than that. They want to know that you truly understand *their* business culture. They want to know that partnering with you will bring them great benefits that they are currently doing without. Don't just tell them about your passion; show them your passion. Your goal is to make them feel that they simply must partner with you!

After the initial meeting, realize that the object of your desire is vetting you and your company just as you are vetting them and theirs. In an internal meeting to assess the results and insights of the first encounter with a potential customer, investor, or stakeholder, ask tough questions. Is the object of your courtship a risk taker in the same way you are? Are they willing to try new methods, procedures, and processes? Are they as open to change as you are? What kind of dance partners would you be? Sometimes, after ample, honest interior debate, you may come to the conclusion that a closer relationship would be inadvisable. It happens! When it does, it's best to back off and direct your energy elsewhere. This is infinitely preferable to moving forward with a doomed relationship. Compatibility is so important. Don't forge ahead if you are certain that you and your potential customer, investor, or stakeholder don't share it.

If you do, however, you must also develop and maintain a vibrant outreach effort. Outreach in this context is just what you'd expect it to be: making use of social media to sustain and nurture relationships. Creating successful, sustainable outreach efforts requires research and a strong understanding of how to optimize search engine use and experience. Always remember that each outreach effort, or campaign, is different. The more research you do for each campaign, the more likely it is that your campaign will meet with success.

Here are some ways that you can make that happen:

Perhaps the most important thing you can do to bond with a potential customer, investor, or stakeholder is offer terrific value. This can take many shapes, including: providing expertise in a field that is important to the other person; offering reports, studies, or accumulated data compiled by your own business; arranging an introduction to another business or possible supporter. Remember that you and your business have assets that can be useful to your partners.

It greatly improves your research if you work with the data from your own and your potential customer's websites. Failure to do this often leads to greater failures. Fortunately, a number of tools are available to assist the entrepreneur in this effort. Backlinks and mentions fill out a performance chart of both your business and the one you may be interested in partnering with, and they deepen your understanding of each other and improve your chances of enjoying a successful collaboration.

Here are some tools that can help. Remember that the technology is always changing, so be sure to keep abreast of those developments:

- Majestic SEO (search engine optimization) helps to look up backlinks, metrics, backlink volume, topical exploration, and mentions.
- BuzzStream is excellent for relationship building and public relations.
- SharedCount provides a way to lasso social metrics on bulk URLs, and it's free!
- Scribe can operate from your WordPress dashboard and provides you with the opportunity to perform in-depth social and keyword research.

We've looked at recognizing and creating potential in beneficial relationships from many angles in this chapter, and it seems right to wrap up by acknowledging the spiritual component that pulses at the heart of every entrepreneur. In the following quote, the wonderful late Irish writer John O'Donohue talks about the soul's emergence and its striving to reach its fullest potential. When an entrepreneur succeeds in this spiritual realm, too, she is even more successful and powerful. This is from O'Donohue's book *Anam Cara: A Book of Celtic Wisdom*: "Once the soul awakens, the search begins and you can never go back. From then on, you are inflamed with a special longing that will never again let you linger in the lowlands of complacency and partial fulfillment. The eternal makes you urgent. You are loath to let compromise or the threat of danger hold you back from striving toward the summit of fulfillment."

6

PRACTICE IN NETWORKING

"Mix, Mingle, Glow. Stretch beyond your own comfort zone to speak with, sit with, and start conversations with people whom you do not know. Take the initiative to help other people capture the spotlight and shine." –Susan C. Young, *The Art of Action: 8 Ways to Initiate and Activate Forward Momentum for Positive First Impact*

Isn't this a great way to begin the practice of networking? "Mix, Mingle, Glow?" I like that Young makes the point that networking helps others shine. Sometimes eager entrepreneurs, especially early in their own development, forget this truth. It's what you can do for others. Attend to that, and what they'll do for you will soon become apparent. Usually, you will like the results.

It's good to remember, now and then, that social networks haven't been around all that long. In the eighties and early nineties, a lot of businesspeople were still working the phones, and using snail mail and early email campaigns. Remember fax machines? Then social networks were brought into organizational theory discussions and studies, and the entire global business landscape changed forever. It changed forever and mostly for the better. Who among us would really like to return to those "good ol' days" when what you accomplish now in hours took days, weeks, months? Yes, I thought so.

To the entrepreneur and her business, of course, the first important social network is her own workplace. People who work together form close, personal working relationships. Some of these even extend outside the workplace. These relationships are the bedrock of any company's culture. Intra-office email makes the sharing of information easy and instantaneous among managers and staff. Projects are more efficiently coordinated and carried out, which makes outside networks more successful and vibrant. This internal network can even give your company competitive advantages over other companies.

By the first decade of the twenty-first century, social networks had become critical to entrepreneurial planning and every other aspect of daily business life. The time and money spent on developing and sustaining social networks quickly became seen as smart investments, even necessary ones. And the hub for social networking is the website.

Some argue that an entrepreneur should build a good website before even opening an office or any place of business. This is OK advice, though if you follow it, you'll need a website that is very flexible and changeable. Inevitably, you'll need to make many changes in the first few years of doing business, then regularly forever after. How regularly depends on the kind of business you have. Whatever kind of business it is, though, everyone who works there should understand that she or he is expected to be capable of accessing the site and performing assigned tasks with its support. If one is practicing social networking, one must be fluent in the company's website. The website is like your social network calling card and research center, and it is the nerve center of your social network practice. It's where products, programs, studies, research, sales, and marketing occur nonstop. The company's evolving practice of social networking will involve these areas and more in the course of conducting business.

Because the practice of networking is a human practice—a desire to create and nurture beneficial community—the entrepreneur must consider the ethics of the work being done and the manner in which it is being done. A high degree of trust and a willingness to share knowledge is essential. Safeguards must be in place to prevent unscrupulous activities from sabotaging partnerships, collaborations, and the business itself. Is anyone being hurt by what the social network is doing? Embracing a code of ethics may be among the most important requirements for all parties taking steps to embrace the practice of social networks.

The benefits of social networking are undeniable. The practice of social networks allows participants to collect more information, awareness, knowledge, advice, and ideas than they might otherwise have collected. Social network practice also gives access to more resources. Three case studies published by I. Davies in the *Journal of Business Ethics* in 2009 documented three benefits of the practice of social networks. The first benefit is a competitive advantage in which the company projects size to a market while in fact remaining small. In other words, the company appears to be bigger than it actually is. The second benefit involves intellectual development. This occurs when intellectual value is shared with many organizations across a wide variety of fields. The third benefit is ideological development through ideological networks of like-minded participants.

Never far from our understanding of and work with social networking is its embodiment of community, of friendship. Would it surprise you to learn that this concept of friendship in social networking actually has an ancient origin? Well, it does. There is a real, traceable connection between networking and Aristotle's three types of friendship.

Aristotle was an ancient Greek philosopher and scientist. A graduate of Plato's Academy, Aristotle proposed the existence of three kinds of friendship: utilitarian, emotional, and virtuous. By applying these categories to social networking, we come up with the three types of networking that people today are most familiar with. Let's consider each of them.

The utilitarian networking model refers to networking practices that occur with the goal of obtaining economic benefits and advantages. This type of networking also includes acquiring power, and insulating oneself from hostile actions. Entrepreneurs use this model to maintain relationships with established customers. They know that it is always cheaper to keep existing customers than to find new customers. Employees use this model to network for better clients and contracts, and even promotions and better jobs. It's also the preferred method for collecting advice and research results.

Emotional networking is most similar to what Aristotle called "friendship for pleasure." In emotional networking, participants are primarily looking for happy, friendly exchanges with other participants. Affection, warmth, and pride are frequently felt by participants of emotional networking, and participants usually share a lot of beliefs, interests, and goals.

The third type is called virtuous networking. If that sounds highfalutin, well, it is in a way. This is the most empathetic type of social network practice. Participants in this type of social networking operate from a strong foundation of moral awareness. The way they go about networking—in other words, doing business—always takes into consideration the feelings and needs of others. Virtuous networkers also look for ways to use the network for causes that benefit culture and society. So, virtuous networkers may create and participate in campaigns that, for example, dig water wells for African villages or build community gardens for low-income neighborhoods or raise funds for a children's hospital.

It should be clear from these three types of social networking that participants run a greater risk of being taken advantage of in utilitarian and emotional networking, while in virtuous networking one is more likely to encounter qualities such as truthfulness, loyalty, justice, and generosity. Aristotle described it in this way: "Those who love each other for their utility do not love each other for themselves but in virtue of some good which they get from each other. So too with those who love for the sake of pleasure." As we've seen, virtuous networking embodies respect and benevolent action; the common good is essential to virtuous networking. Participants usually give more than they expect to receive.

There are four qualities one should strive to inject into the practice of virtuous, ethical social networking. One is the intention of sharing goals and activities in a selfless, collaborative way. A second is a free and willing exchange of knowledge, learning, and information. A third is the beneficial expression of power, participant to participant. The fourth is presence—

awareness of the behavioral influence exerted within the group by the various participants. This should be done with an eye toward balancing these influences in beneficial ways. Honest goals, generosity, and good faith (in other words, trust) go a long way toward realizing the promise of beneficial social networking.

Misconduct, of course, can and will undermine and destroy any social network. That is why creating an ethical foundation for social networks is so important. Still, everyone knows that misconduct in various guises is rampant in social networking. Corruption and bribery are blatant forms of misconduct, but more subtle forms of misconduct can be equally devastating. Consider those cases of illegal insider trading that hit the news from time to time.

Cronyism is another form of misconduct that can damage a social network and its participants. Most often, cronyism in social networks takes the form of a participant rewarding an unqualified participant with a job or opportunity that eventually leads to profit and advantage to both participants. In the pre–social network days, "nepotism" best described this type of behavior. Unfortunately, social networks can, in the early stages at least, shield cronyism from the general public's view.

All that matters is this: that one pay attention. Be present and generous of spirit! Trust and expect trust, and all will be well in your practice of social networking. It is about the people you choose to work with, yes, but it's also about the way they conduct themselves and you conduct yourself. Also, it always comes back to your intention.

In a 2016 article, Ada Pang, owner of People Bloom Counseling in Redmond, Washington, shared her goal when attending a social networking event: "When I go to any networking event," wrote Pang, "I don't plan to get clients. Rather, I am curious about what others are doing and I want to learn from them. If I get a referral from them, awesome. If I don't, hopefully I've made an impression and I can be a resource in the future." Remember that patience is essential in practicing and building a successful network.

Amy Fortney Parks, the executive director of WISE Mind Solutions, LLC, in Northern Virginia, describes herself as a lifelong talker whose sixth-grade teacher once accused her of having "diarrhea of the mouth." Were you such a kid? Are you a grown-up who loves to talk? Or are you terrified by the prospect of getting up in front of a crowd and talking about yourself and your business?

Fortney Parks is an advocate of the belief that talking spreads valuable information, not just hot air. Fortney Parks encourages others to get out and talk to community groups, reading groups, church groups, anywhere you can get yourself invited to stand up and share your life and business experience with truth and humor (humor is a great sales device). At the same time, she urges people to collect as much information as they can about others. "When you speak in front of a group," says Fortney Parks, "you have instant credibility, because someone has chosen YOU to hold the attention of the audience. They can trust you." Fortney Parks goes on to say that when you speak in public you get to reveal your personality. This is what people want. They want to know about the person whose event they've invested their time in.

When you speak in public, when you overcome reluctance or shyness and put yourself out there, you also have a chance to promote your business. A smart thing to do is to share testimonials from your clients. As the audience listens, they imagine themselves enjoying similar successes with you—*because* of you. Listeners will get the impression that you deliver results, and they will be grateful for the opportunity to meet you.

And when you do speak in public, Fortney Parks points out, set aside some time for immediate follow-up. Yes, talk and communicate and learn, but also, follow up. "I block out two to three hours after EVERY talk I give," says Fortney Parks, "to follow up and write thank you notes."

An Exercise in Practicing Social Networking

In writing, imagine the ideal social network for you. List or write in paragraph form everything you can think of. What descriptors would fit the participants in your ideal social network? What interests would you have in common? What goals?

As an entrepreneur concerned with marketing, what social network practices might work best for you and your business? You need visibility. You need to be trusted by customers and potential customers. What can you do to achieve those goals?

One thing you can do is to make sure you are crystal clear about your theme or themes. For example, Airbnb promotes its brand by showcasing its most outrageous and creative rentals worldwide on Instagram. The listings are current and available, and one can actually click right through to the listing's special landing page. Another example is Casper. On Twitter, Casper tweets hilarious messages all the time that all spin around a single activity. What is it? Sleep! What better focus for a mattress company? And as we've seen before, humor is a great way to connect with others and drive sales. And let's not forget Facebook. Microsoft uses Facebook to announce news, new releases, and events involving the whole industry, and to spread its internal and external blog posts.

So, how does an entrepreneur practice social networking like Airbnb, Casper, Microsoft, and other successful companies? An entrepreneur can encourage others to get involved by inviting them to share with the company their own (user-generated) content so the company can post it on Instagram. The entrepreneur might also want to engage in humor—not all the time, but often enough. Humor works! An entrepreneur can also engage an audience by asking questions. One can ask questions on many social networks such as Facebook, Twitter, Instagram, LinkedIn, and others. Whole Foods Market did this recently with a question: "Can you guess the secret ingredient?"

On Instagram Stories, an entrepreneur can take customers on a behind-the-scenes tour of the company or business. These visits make it easier for viewers to identify with the company and the people who work for it. Strong visual images and snappy, colorful videos posted on social networks also score well with visiting viewers. And don't forget to post shots of your products and customer testimonials. This evidence plants what you do *and* the business's accomplishments in the minds of new visitors.

Whatever you choose to do, you must never lose sight of the fact that consistency is vital to the maintenance and success of your brand and its voice. It is wise to keep in mind an Oracle report finding that 43 percent of social media users interact with a particular brand in order to receive a direct response to a specific issue or a question. This is a useful statistic, don't you think? So is the next one, but it's also scary. Sixty-six percent of internet visitors, at one time or another, have felt misled and deceived by a brand's social media posts, content, or videos. Yes, one must be so careful these days! If you alter the voice of your brand, you'll lose the trust of your audience. Forty-one percent of participants in social networks have decided to unfollow brands because they posted information that these followers found unhelpful and irrelevant. As an entrepreneur practicing social networking, you must walk a tightrope between self-promotion and diversity of content. Consistency is what you want, always consistency as you highlight your brand voice. When you are practicing social networking, be consistent in your replies, the call-to-action phrases you use, captions, social media biographies, direct messages, visuals (and the text on visuals), ads, promotions, and hashtags.

Next, avoid trendy slogans, slang, and internet-speak. You can't win using these words. To some you'll seem out of touch. Others will think you're acting phony, and some will accuse you of being cynical for a profit. Mistakes like these embarrass people. They think you're out of touch when it comes to demographics, or that you're culturally insensitive, or that you're pretending to be something you're not or represent something you do not believe in. If you think I'm exaggerating, consider this statistic: 71.3 percent of visitors on social networks have unfollowed a brand because they found that brand embarrassing. It's a lot easier than you think to come off looking like a square on social networks, and when you look like a square, well, that's the direct opposite of looking cool.

Whether you are just starting up or are already actively engaged and seeking ways to improve your social networking performance and results, there are always things you can do to get better. Even when you think you are contributing a great deal to the social network conversations you're a part of, think of ways to contribute even more. Try to please the people who are listening to you!

The best way to do this, of course, is by being entertaining. I know, easier said than done, especially if you are inherently shy, the quiet type. I know many entrepreneurs who have joined Toastmasters to develop their skills as public speakers. Often, this leads to greater self-confidence in social networking, too. You might try it! It might feel scary at first, but it does work. Or you might consider joining a reading group that includes lots of opinionated discussion. This venue can also serve to bring you gently out of your shell. Even if you feel comfortable putting yourself out there, being entertaining is a tricky proposition. How many times have you observed entertaining people, or people who thought they were entertaining, who were actually obnoxious? That's an awful spot to find yourself in! So, you always have to be listening carefully to yourself to make sure you are actually entertaining, and not a pain in the you-know-where. When in doubt, run your social networking comments by some trusted associates. That's why you have them. Rely on their judgment and make use of their advice.

As you practice social networking, you will also want to excite, even inspire, your audience. If you inspire those listening to you, they will respond with more insights and chatter of their own, and that's what you want—more conversation and more engagement.

Here is something that seems so obvious yet is easy to forget: When others are talking in your social networks, they're often talking about you. What are they really saying? Are you paying adequate attention to nuance and tone? Are you interpreting context correctly? Think about this: How can you successfully communicate with others if you don't understand what they're really saying about you and your work? Some people have a real block when it comes to hearing what others think of them. If you are one of those people, again, reach out to your trusted associates for feedback and guidance. They're with you to help you. Listen carefully to those talking about you and your business and learn from them. Sift through the commentary and make changes as needed. Ignoring what others say and failing to assimilate their good suggestions is a bad strategy in business, always.

In your social networks, you will also want to deliver as much information about research and resources to your fellow participants as you can. No doubt you are practicing social networking because you're interested in receiving more research and finding new resources that will aid your business. Everyone else is practicing social networking for the same reasons. Remember an earlier truth we discussed, about how virtuous networkers give more to others than they expect to receive themselves? If you do this, you'll find that more will come to you than you imagine.

In retrospect, these suggestions seem self-evident, yet in the rush and fury of daily business lives, it's easy to forget or overlook them. One does so at one's peril. The particulars of social networking are always unique, but the general rules that govern success are surprisingly straightforward and almost universal. Be consistent, and be committed to providing beneficial experiences for everyone you encounter in your practice of social networking. If you just do that, social networking success will come.

Entrepreneurs, no matter who they are and what they do, must be able to create and sustain beneficial working relationships with those who can help them do a better job and reach their goals. I knew an entrepreneur who was so busy he didn't have time for practicing social networking, which he disdainfully saw as doing favors for and seeking favors from total strangers. He failed to embrace the honesty of social networks, and cynically rejected them instead. Need I tell you that he is no longer an entrepreneur?

Earlier, we looked at social networking as an Aristotelian model. (Can you imagine how much fun Aristotle would have on the internet if he were alive today?) Let's consider another model for social networking. Imagine that there are three categories of social networking: operational, personal, and strategic.

The purpose of operational social networking is to get work done quickly and well and maintain the functions the group needs to keep going. Most of the contacts in this type of social networking are internal, and they are most concerned with what needs to be done *now*. The key contacts in these networks are no secret. Your organization and the tasks at hand dictate who needs to be doing what. Through all procedures and processes, the goal is to develop depth of understanding and to create strong, enduring relationships.

The purpose of personal social networking is to strengthen personal development and professional development. In this type of network, you are often referring others to new contacts, research, and good information. While contacts are mostly internal in operational social networking, contacts are mostly external in personal social networking. Your key contacts are also more discretionary than they are in operational social networking because it isn't always certain who is most relevant for the tasks at hand. Personal social networking is focused on reaching new contacts who can offer new referrals.

Strategic social networking focuses on future priorities and other challenges that have not yet materialized. In consideration of such inevitable issues, this network must include stakeholder support. Contacts in strategic social networking are internal and external; they are all focused on the future, not the here and now. As with personal social networks, relevant key contacts here aren't always clearly visible. The key to strategic social networking is creating leverage, or outside-inside links.

Operational networking comes easily for most managers-entrepreneurs, but even then, many have trouble connecting with some of the participants that actually help them get things done. Entrepreneurs can rely too exclusively on operational networking, and not enough on the other two forms of social networks. By focusing too much on the interior workings of one's own company, the manager-entrepreneur fails to plan adequately for the future and even has a claustrophobic, skewed view of the present.

It's then that the entrepreneur must broaden her focus and embrace personal social networking. Who are your soulmates outside your own organization? That's what you need to look for as you move on to personal social networking. It may take time to find them. Some entrepreneurs are resistant to broadening their network of casual acquaintances when time is already at a premium. Isn't this spreading oneself too thin? Not at all! Important referrals will come to you. You might even find coaches and mentors through personal social networking. Personal development is a byproduct of personal social networking, which itself provides a platform for leaping into strategic networking.

I knew a woman, a key figure at a start-up publishing company, who was painfully shy. When given time to prepare for presentations, she was fine, but she stumbled terribly through all spontaneous interactions inside and outside the company. She knew her future was limited unless she addressed her shyness, so she decided to become proactive, and began to force herself to attend the kinds of social get-togethers that she had always avoided. She even read up on the people she knew would be there. This background checking helped to put her at ease. Gradually, she became more fluid in social situations, more confident, and this translated to being infinitely more effective at her job. Her participation in personal social networking resulted in many new referrals.

This woman's experience is far from unusual. In companies all over the world, entrepreneurs struggle to some extent with their social skills and social networking skills. Organizational goals are best served when these skills are developed and polished. When they are, strategic networking becomes an exciting additional social network platform.

The more successful an entrepreneur becomes, the more she transitions from a position of functional management to a position of true leadership. She begins to see that there are bigger strategic issues she needs to grasp if she and the company are to continue to grow and become successful. Relationships outside and inside the company, many of them beyond the control of the leader, become the very lifeblood of the company. These connections benefit the leader as she determines how she can best contribute to the big picture. Eventually she evolves to the point where she knows exactly when to alter her perspective, acknowledging what is important and allocating her time and energy accordingly. For example, strategic social networking may include strategic projects that address the future, deep discussions with other leaders outside and inside the business, building new teams to meet new challenges, and advancing new programs, projects, and business case developments. These efforts create an invaluable support system for evolving entrepreneurs.

Becoming a true leader who feels comfortable in strategic social marketing requires flexibility. It's like shedding an old skin. Leaders become successful only when they prove capable of changing their perspectives and embracing new realities. They understand what they must do to contribute and add value to the efforts and bottom line of the company. The more a leader performs like a leader, the more she shifts from objectives that are on the table to objectives that will be on the table in the future. This leader will develop new skills as needed and will be able to work well with diverse groups that bring a host of different skill sets to the process of successfully meeting the goals of the business. Business history is packed with stories of managers and executives who are "suddenly" stripped of responsibilities or reassigned to other tasks, tasks which feel like a demotion, a slap on the wrist, or worse. Usually, the reason behind such a change is the fact that the person failed to anticipate shifts in priorities and in the markets for which she was responsible. Most often, demotions like this occur when leaders decide that the executive or manager lacks a wide understanding about where the business is headed. In other words, the manager is perceived to be lacking in strategic social networking skills.

This lack of foresight can sink a leader so quickly! One day a manager is sailing along with her team. She feels good about her

relationships with her team members. She basks in the successes the team

has achieved. She feels good about the company and her role in it. Then,

the next day, *wham*! She is stripped of her responsibilities and is reassigned.

What happened?

What happened is, she failed to read the obvious signs that were all

around her. Perhaps she even ignored colleagues who gently made attempts

to warn her. She remained obstinately clueless, allowing herself to become

too insulated from the company culture and the industry itself. Burrowing

into a comfort zone is extremely dangerous. When it occurs, internal

counseling can be of great assistance to the affected manager. Talking to

someone wiser, someone in the company who possesses a broader

perspective, can help the manager realize what's been going on; that mentor

can help her adjust, and help her form new priorities. This is one of the

many functions a good mentor performs.

But many managers who burrow into this comfort zone are

resistant to change. They tend to blame others, insisting that their demotion

is a result of inner politics. They point fingers at others. They claim that

their problems result from a deep, systemic dysfunction within the

company, yet the deepest dysfunction most often lies within the individual

pointing the finger. Needless to say, these managers do not enjoy a long life with the company.

People who withdraw from the business culture like this do not understand, as good entrepreneurs and social networkers do, that strategic networking is very much about leverage. What is leverage? It's the ability to gather the resources and support you need from one sector and apply it toward success in another. Indirect influence works wonders in such efforts. For example, a member within the network might influence someone outside the network to take an action that the network deems necessary. This is tricky for many beginning entrepreneurs, who tend to spend more time meeting organizational daily demands than developing their strategic social networks—which is the worst thing they can do.

Vibrant strategic social networks can clear up logjams and personnel misunderstandings, and help lead the company into a better future. Good strategic networks will also reinforce entrepreneurs and managers and keep them in the loop, where they must be if they hope to reach their goals and succeed.

In the real world, operational, personal, and strategic networks are not exclusive: They blend together in ways that are always pushing the entrepreneur to expand his comfort zone. A manager I know in real estate vacations every year, signing up for fly-fishing expeditions that bring him together, for a week or two, with people from industries that have nothing to do with his own. On his last trip, he was bivouacked with the professional guide (whom he knew from earlier trips) as well as an owner of a construction company, a lawyer, a manager of a software company, a college professor, and a physician. All were there for the fishing, of course, yet they also benefited from exposure to one another. How? By trading stories. The lawyer's anecdote about getting a difficult customer to follow through and meet deadlines dictated by court appearances resonated with the real estate manager. The professor and the physician hit it off and enjoyed several animated conversations about their students and patients. In effect, a personal social network had also became operational and strategic, as the shared stories had one common element—customer relations.

Manager-entrepreneurs need to first believe in the importance of social networking in order to practice it well. Intuition and judgment serve the entrepreneur well if she opens herself up to both and is willing to listen. Try to think of social networking as all of the things you could get done on down time. Traveling for work or pleasure presents splendid opportunities to practice social networking. What one hears, what one observes, makes one a better manager, and a better entrepreneur.

Exercise: Practicing Social Networking

Take a walk in the woods or your local park. Tune in to your surroundings. What do the ants on that mound look like, and what are they doing? Describe the scene in a notebook. Can you name the flowers you pass by on your walk? The shrubs and the trees? Choose a tree that draws you near. Respectfully rest your hand on its bark. Do you feel a gentle pulse, even a surge, of energy running up your arm? Close your eyes; feel and listen. What is the tree telling you? Tune in! You are practicing social networking with the tree, and with your surroundings.

Social networking only works when you use it. The best time is not when you desperately need to fix something—the best time is *all* the time. The entrepreneurs and managers who discover this early and never forget it are the ones who succeed. Those who stop short, network sporadically, and inevitably fall behind are the ones who fail. What kind of entrepreneur and manager to do you want to be?

"Building relationships is not about transactions—it's about connections. The term 'networking' is simply another way to think about how to start a relationship. Our relationships are our network. Building fruitful and lasting relationships starts with abandoning the conventional 'me'-based thoughts that are so prevalent in the business world and so easy to slip into our personal lives." –Michelle Tillis Lederman, author of *The 11 Laws of Likability: Relationship Networking... Because People Do Business with People They Like.*

"People bond when they are having fun. Where attention goes, energy flows." –Itzik Amiel, author of *The Attention Switch.*

7

POWER OF NETWORKING

"You can have everything in life you want if you will just help enough other people get what they want." –Zig Ziglar

"Networking is marketing. Marketing yourself, marketing your uniqueness, marketing what you stand for." –Christine Comaford-Lynch

Many new entrepreneurs find it more than a little scary to embrace the true power of networking, but what most of those are truly frightened of is their own innate power. It's a big step and a small step for anyone to take, yet once it is taken, opportunity blossoms.

Never have there been more communication channels open to the entrepreneur than there are today. Power resides in relationships, in discovering them, in nurturing them, and in embracing the collaborative opportunities they present.

In days gone by, creating powerful networking depended on direct mail campaigns—we're talking snail mail here. It depended on making phone calls and, when possible, showing up for face-to-face visits. It took days, weeks, even months to accomplish what one can get done in a few hours today. Social networks today are truly global; or rather, they should be. The entrepreneur who has realized her own power knows that the power emanates from within herself; once she feeds the power of others through powerful social networking, she then receives surges of greater power from those relationships. It's a beautiful, fluid process that every LEAP SEVEN practitioner has perfected.

Janelle came up with a great idea for a new app that would help people more easily learn a foreign language. A gifted programmer, she perfected her discovery by working on it during evenings at home after her day job. She tried it out on close friends, some of them also programmers, and the feedback was all positive, even glowing. With help from some of these friends, Janelle researched the field and found that there was definitely a niche for her product, and a potentially profitable one at that. In her spare time, she created a functional website but did not yet go live with it. She was still planning, and she planned a lot! She planned so much that her closest friends began to ask her what was taking so long. She told them she just wanted to be ready, but in their eyes, she'd been ready for some time.

The truth was, Janelle was paralyzed by fear. She doubted that she could overcome her natural shyness to build the networks she knew she would need in order to be successful. It took months before she would admit this to her close friends, and months after that before she finally launched her website, invested some of her modest savings, and went public.

Because Janelle was an excellent planner, she did not fall prey to the urge to go too fast too soon. She advanced methodically and enlisted the help of some close friends in the process of creating her social network. The plan and its execution were successful. In time, Janelle's company thrived, so much so that a major software firm opened negotiations to buy her out for seven-plus figures.

Not every new entrepreneur will match Janelle's success, and that's OK. Success is relative. Many entrepreneurs find their true power in creating a business that will never be gigantic but will always be successful if properly managed. Size does not dictate power. This is true even in social networking. Powerful social networking can be done on any scale.

Really, didn't you become powerful as a social networker the moment you began to gather and create a list of emails? That's the beginning for everybody, and the process never stops. You've probably expanded and expanded your list and discovered, joined, and created other lists (or networks, as we call them). As you've grown, so has your power. You've learned that your networks can serve a variety of purposes, even quite personal ones.

A friend of mine saw a large dog sideswiped by a car. The car kept going as the dog lay on the street in pain. My friend ran to the dog and comforted him. There were no cuts that she could see, but she knew the dog was seriously injured. With as much tenderness as she could muster, she managed to lift the dog into her car and drive him to the nearest vet just a few blocks away. Inside, she explained what had happened, and the vet brought the dog in and immediately attended to him. The diagnosis? The dog had a broken front left leg. There were two options—put the dog down, or set the leg and put it in a cast. The dog wore no identification tags and no one at the vet recognized him. The immediate decision of what to do rested with my friend—who, two hours earlier, hadn't even know that the dog existed! She's responsible, though, my friend (who was now the dog's friend, too!). She asked the vet to save the dog, to set his broken leg. An hour later, the dog was resting quietly, and he would spend the next few days at the vet's office, where he could be watched.

This is a good story, but what does it have to do with networking? Let's get to that now.

The dog was temporarily saved, but what was my friend going to do with him? Saving the dog cost hundreds of dollars, money my friend did not have. She decided to do two things. First, she took photos of the dog and posted them all over the neighborhood. That is primitive networking at its best! Next, she launched an online funding campaign to raise a thousand dollars for the dog's vet bill, while at the same time appealing to potential donors to consider adopting the dog if an owner did not step forward.

As it turned out, an owner did appear. After three days, a distraught young woman, having seen one of my friend's posters on a telephone pole, rushed to the vet's office and was reunited with the dog, whose named turned out to be Jack. When my friend met her, Jack's owner was grateful and nervous. She was nervous because she was unemployed and couldn't afford the vet bill, either. My friend reassured her, suggesting they wait and see how the funding campaign went. Four days later, the campaign met my friend's goal! In fact, $1,135 had been raised! Once again, because they had been asked and made aware of a situation, compassionate people came through. Ask and ye shall receive.

This story had a happy ending in large part because my friend was willing to get involved. She was willing to exercise her imagination, solve problems, and put herself out there. What she accomplished happened because of her power, because of her willingness to seize opportunity and make something positive out of it. How different the story might have turned out had she simply ignored the accident and moved along. But that's not my friend's style. Her style embodies much more power and more success. Because she asked, she found others who were willing to help her and the dog. This is a personal anecdote of power networking on a small scale. Networking at its finest.

OK, I imagine many of you thinking, "So, power networking is really important to my business and career—not to mention my life! But is there a game plan for power networking? How do I organize and get going?"

Fluidity is an important feature in any business plan. Without it, business gets stuck. It's generally true that the very first step in power networking is to give good value before you ever expect to receive good value. Whether it's with advice, services, or products, be generous! Think of the anecdote of my friend and the dog. She got involved because she was compassionate, responsible, and generous. She didn't expect any reward. It really ought to be that way in business, too. When it isn't, relationships gets off on the wrong foot and often never recover. Do good for others, and good things will come to you.

An easy but powerful step in building your social networks is to seek and ask for introductions to new contacts who can advance your efforts. How can you identify those? Intuition, research, and the advice of contacts you already know and trust! Look people up on Facebook, on LinkedIn, on Instagram, and elsewhere. Ask your friends, family, and colleagues for suggestions. You know that adding strong referrals to your networks will help you grow your business, so… collect names and make contact! When you do, invite the people you connect with out to coffee or tea or lunch. Be concise and clear about what you do and why you would like to work with the person.

In power networking, never lose sight of the fact that you seek real personal connections, and not just numbers in a database. I've known many entrepreneurs who have made the mistake of thinking that collecting business cards equals successful networking. It's not enough to collect business cards and add the names and addresses to your database. A lot of people will resent hearing from you if that's all you've done. In fly fishing, you don't find success by randomly casting your line all over the river or the lake. You look for telltale signs—a hatch of insects above a calm pool, or unusual bubbles occurring in a pocket of the river. You don't get a strike every time, but the more often you cast in promising spots, the more strikes you will have. Personal connections are better than impersonal connections. After you meet a new contact, write down that person's strengths and what you might hope for in working with her.

Once you've made contact, be sure to follow up. Not often enough to drive the person crazy, but often enough to demonstrate that you are diligent and persistent; in other words, someone who might be safe and fun to do business with. How do you identify such people? How can you be sure? A friend always assigns a number to a new person he meets, writing the number down on the back of that person's card. If the number is six or better, he adds a few quick notes detailing the topics that came up in their introductory conversation. The next day, he emails the person, managing to work in a personal reference that is friendly and appropriate. In this email, he might even offer to connect the new person with someone who might be helpful to her. My friend also commits to staying in touch with the new person on a regular basis. Of course, frequency of contact will in part be determined by the response he gets from these initial emails. Yet it's a good rule to keep in touch regularly. It really does establish confidence and ease between two people. So be sure to set aside a certain amount of time each day to work your social networks and stick to your schedule. Don't get tired or bored and forget! If you do, people will swiftly forget you!

The more you learn about a person, the easier it becomes to stay in touch and deepen the relationship. What does the person care about? What are her or his passions? Perhaps he would love tickets to a basketball game. Maybe she loves to play golf and would welcome an invitation. Tickets to a hit theatrical show might be in order, or a gift card, or just a simple invitation to meet for tea or coffee. Maybe a walk in the park would be fun and helpful to both of you. The point is, there are plenty of opportunities to connect and do things together.

It's great for business—and your general health—to open up to people, and to like people. Yet one should be sensitive to how easily one settles into a comfort zone. It's just human nature that we tend to enjoy spending time with people who are more like us than unlike us. There is a tendency to gravitate toward people of the same gender and level of training, with similar educations and shared ethnicity. This is OK as a starting point, but the successful and sensitive entrepreneur will evolve beyond this place. That entrepreneur will actively seek diversity in her evolving social networks because she knows that diversity makes her networks stronger. So, push yourself to engage with people you might not normally seek out. Some of them will introduce you to subsets of people you might never have known, and some of them will do great things for you and your business.

In a similar vein, it's wise to think of practicing up *and* down power networking. What do I mean by that? Well, the general tendency in building social networks is to focus on people more advanced than you are. You want to get to where they are! But it is also wise to include people who are younger than you or not as advanced yet. They, too, can provide contacts and insights that may prove valuable to you, and eventually some of them will advance and be on par with you, or even surpass you. Business might be compared to an elevator. Whether you are going up or down, you are meeting many of the same people. So treat everyone well!

Power in social networking relies in part on your social network profiles. Younger people today tend to put way too much personal information online, and it's not wise. Just as you do, others check out your profile before contacting you, and what they find online plays an important part in whether or not they'll want to engage more deeply and do business with you. Don't just accept anyone's friend request: Check her or him out first! What do you have in common? What contacts do you already share? Has the person sent you a personal message or just a form request? A lot of times, it's wise to pass—but respectfully, of course. It damages your reputation if it looks like you're a flake online.

Remember, too, that there is always common ground, no matter how different two people may appear to be. Don't be afraid to ask personal questions about children and favorite activities. And don't simply fall into the trap of being the inquisitor! Ask questions, yet open up about yourself, too. Share your own experiences when appropriate.

This is a lot to keep in mind, I know, but it's easier than it sounds. Once you get started, enthusiasm and curiosity will kick in and spur you onward. ***Power in social networking is not just about getting—it's also about getting to know.*** The more you know, about people, about situations, about other businesses and markets, the more successful you will inevitably become. All you need to do is start emailing and start talking, and others will email and talk back to you. It's like I always tell people who complain in workshops about being stuck and not being able to write: "Here's the secret," I say. "The poet and writer Robert McDowell teaches that all you have to do is put the tip of your pen or pencil to the paper and start moving it. Something will happen. Something will come."

One big thing that will come is opportunity. Opportunity will multiply as your social networks grow. These opportunities may include client leads, partnerships, speaking engagements, seminar teaching offers, writing invitations, joint ventures, sales of assets, partnerships, collaborative community engagement, and invitations to attend conferences. These are just some of the opportunities that will inevitably come your way if you are powerfully developing your social networks in true LEAP SEVEN fashion.

It can't be said enough that it's not *what* you know in business, but *who* you know. The successful entrepreneur needs to call on people all the time for help, guidance, or participation. Successful networking opens doors to influential and powerful people you might otherwise never know. Yet you also need to be discerning, even subtle, to make sure that the people you're in touch with are really the right people to help you reach your goals. I've known many entrepreneurs who have wandered off into back channels and lost vast amounts of time networking, or trying to, with people who couldn't really help them. It's all about the questions you ask others and how well you listen. Does the person you are talking to really know what you need to know? If the answer is yes, great! Enjoy and nurture the developing relationship. If the answer is no, politely and gracefully move on.

Powerful social networking generates advice and balance. A reliable, trusted contact can offer lots of great advice about your business and even about your personal life. This combination often helps strike that sometimes elusive balance between professional and private life.

I knew an entrepreneur who was six years into a successful landscape business. She directed the business and her husband sometimes helped her with projects. Like many beginning entrepreneurs, she launched her business from her home. As the business became more successful, she and her husband decided that they would build a small office up the hill from their house and run the business out of it. This was an exciting and gratifying expansion. Every time she left her home and walked up the hill to her new office, she felt proud of the work she was doing, and felt validated for her choices. Her husband, too, seemed to enjoy the fact that she was able to work so close to home.

This arrangement worked very well for a couple of years, but over time the couple seemed to be growing apart. What was happening? Uncomfortable with the growing distance between them, the woman asked her especially close contacts for advice. A couple of contacts offered to shadow her for a couple of days. What they observed seemed so obvious, yet it had eluded the entrepreneur and her husband altogether! What they saw was that the woman was spending abnormally long hours working. She was even working seven days a week. Why?

This is a common trap for entrepreneurs who either work out of the home or work from an office adjacent to the home. The business is literally so close that it is hard to shut it down every day and walk away. The woman had naturally fallen into the habit of working, working, and then working some more. The job and business were always right in front of her. Her life at work and her life at home had become unbalanced. It got so bad that the marriage itself was threatened.

Fortunately, her trusted contacts intervened with sound advice. They sat down with the entrepreneur and her husband and talked about the need for any businessperson to put the job down at the end of the day and walk away. One shared his own story of almost losing his family to his work. It's a common story.

The woman really had been unaware of the pattern she had fallen into. Her husband had recognized it, but she had made him feel that it was an unwelcome topic. Silences that are allowed to go on and on will often break apart a relationship.

That didn't happen in this story. The woman, on reflection, realized that she loved her business *and* her husband and did not want to lose either one. So, again with the input of her trusted advisors, she created an action plan. It was pretty simple, really: She agreed that no matter what, she would turn off the lights and leave the office for home by six o'clock every night. She also agreed that she would not work weekends, that instead she would take weekend trips with her husband. In the beginning, it wasn't always easy to stick to this plan. What if there was an emergency? What if five thirty didn't feel like a good time to quit for the day? Those days happen! Every now and then, it's OK to work late. Her husband would then volunteer to keep her company in the office and help out if needed. He even brought snacks up to the office for her.

In the long run, things worked out for these two. Thanks to the help from her social networks, this entrepreneur and her husband passed together through one of the many challenges that face entrepreneurs, and they managed to regain their life balance. The business continued to grow and be successful, and so did their marriage, their life partnership. Balance—life balance—is another powerful benefit of social networking.

Through it all, be aware of the need to raise your profile whenever you can. Of course, you will get tired of hobnobbing, of being "on" all the time. That's natural, and that's why you must factor in down time so that you can recharge your battery. Just be consistent with your social schedule. Regularly attend business meetings. Make it to those Rotary Club breakfasts on a fairly regular basis. Sit in on workshops and conferences. Chat up fellow attendees. Be supportive! That genuine support will then come around to you, too.

As you sift through contacts and put together your social networks, be aware of the importance of communing with positive people. Negative people and their negative energy won't just bring *you* down; they can bring down your business, too. You are who you know.

You are also how you act. We hear all the time about the importance of self-confidence, and it frankly scares a lot of people. We all want to be self-confident, yet many of us are shy and retiring. It's scary to put ourselves out there! Yet it's a skill that can be learned, like public speaking. The more you talk to people and socialize, the better you will get at it. In time, almost before you know it, your self-confidence will blossom, and your business will, too.

I've taught classes and workshops and spoken to groups for many years as an entrepreneur and teacher. Early on, I made up for a lack of self-confidence by being super prepared. I wrote out everything! If my talks lacked spontaneity, at least I covered all the bases. But over time, I felt more and more constricted by prepared comments and notes. One day, I took the big leap and spoke without notes. I thought to myself, *You've been doing this for so long! If you don't know this stuff, who does?* That really worked. I discovered that I was able to engage an audience much more effectively than I used to, and the spontaneity created all kinds of magical moments and insights that I—and the people listening—would have missed otherwise.

The satisfaction I derived from this discovery was immeasurable. Even better was my realization that I was proving to be a bigger help to my audience than I had been before. Yes, I had indeed come a long way from my early days of social networking. In the beginning, I was often petrified by the experience, but I stuck with it and slowly got my power marketing legs under me. If someone tells you that social networking gets easier over time, well, they're telling you the truth! Be diligent and persistent and you shall be rewarded. That's a LEAP SEVEN promise.

This is hard to believe when you're first starting out, but you will feel immense satisfaction when you help others. There is really nothing like it. Today my social networks crackle with business owners and workers who are having problems with campaigns, budgets, programs, proposals, staff, planning, investors, customers—you name it! And I am right there with them. The business world is one of constant flux, fascinating challenges, and limitless opportunity. Thanks to social networks, it's easier than ever to reach out to someone and give them the help they need. That feels terrific. It also feels pretty good when someone does that for you, and they will.

As they do, you'll discover that wonderful friendships develop over time. It's natural. You're networking with fellow businesspeople. You all have a lot in common. The help you give each other will sometimes form the foundation for an enduring friendship. Human beings are social animals. We need friends to feel fully realized and happy. Without friends, we're unbalanced in our personal lives and in our business lives. Friends just make the journey sweeter. I've met some of my closest friends on my social networks. You can probably say the same thing, or will be able to soon.

In a 2013 *Los Angeles Times* profile of UC San Diego professor James Fowler, journalist Joe Yogerst wrote, "Although social media can't replace in-person relationships, Fowler believes that its power to bring people in closer contact with strangers and spread information quickly can create important new group-level efforts like crowd-sourcing (think: Wikipedia or Kickstarter) and large-scale coordination (think: flash mobs or Arab Spring protests)."

This excellent insight comments on the power of social networking in a larger context. At its core, social networking is intensely personal. It's almost basic in that way. Yet social networking also affects diverse cultures and societies. Social networking is an effective device that can change politics, governments, social attitudes, and cultural characteristics. If you doubt this assertion, just ask a teenager. Here is one commenting on the importance of social networking in *HuffPost*: "Teenagers like myself are among the top users of most social media platforms on the Internet. Whether it's updating a Facebook status, fitting a joke into 140 characters or uploading a picture of our lunch to Instagram, we are on the Internet a lot. Social media is a huge part of our culture."

Would you like more evidence? Consider Hugh Evans. Evans, largely using social networking, launched a movement that seeks to galvanize "global citizens." These are people who identify themselves as members of the human race, rather than members of a particular country or state or tribe. Evans inspires and encourages others to act against poverty, climate change, gender inequality, and other global blights that need to be addressed by all of us. "These are ultimately global issues," Evans says in his TED Talk, "and they can only be solved by global citizens demanding global solutions from their leaders." Here is a link to Evans' uplifting and challenging speech in its entirety:

https://www.ted.com/talks/hugh_evans_what_does_it_mean_to_be_a_cit
izen_of_the_world?referrer=playlist-the_power_of_social_media.

Or you may really enjoy listening to this hilarious four-minute TED

Talk by Reddit founder Alexis Ohanian (perhaps better known now as the

lucky husband of the fabulous Serena Williams). In his talk, Ohanian tells

the tale of a humpback whale's rise to web stardom. Appropriately, the talk

is called "How to Make a Splash in Social Media," and here is the link to it:

https://www.ted.com/talks/alexis_ohanian_how_to_make_a_splash_in_so
cial_media?referrer=playlist-the_power_of_social_media.

Powerful social networking is literally saving lives now, too. Just

take a look at the medical field to see how. We're all reading a lot these days

about the opioid epidemic. It's a global crisis that has ruined millions of

lives and killed many people. Social networks, though, are making accessible

more and more information about treatments and options for opioid

addicts. I know a woman whose life was saved by a medically based social

network. After a car accident, she became addicted to opioids and almost

lost her life. For three years, she barely left her home. She lost her job. Her

relationship with her husband was in tatters, and she became increasingly

abusive to anyone who tried to help her. It got so bad that she seriously

contemplated suicide. At that point, one of her few remaining friends suggested she visit an opioid addicts' chat room. Of course, she resisted the suggestion, but one night, for whatever reason, she broke down and gave it a try. At least she did not have to leave her home to get there!

She had convinced herself that she was all alone, that no one could ever understand what she was going through, but what she discovered in that chat room changed—maybe even saved—her life. Surprise! There were others just like her. She was suddenly chatting back and forth with women and men who knew exactly what she was going through. Forcing herself to get online and enter that chat room turned out to be her first significant step in the long road to recovery. Today, she makes no bones about it: The people she met in that chat room and in other chat rooms over the course of several months saved her life. Because of their empathy and good advice, she was able, finally, to get the treatment she needed. A year later, she was more or less back to her old self, able to leave the house with ease. She was even working again. And at the heart of her remarkable recovery? Social networks!

We've seen how social networking casts a wide, diverse, global net, and to refocus our microscope we remind ourselves that social networking is absolutely essential to our businesses, too. When worked wisely, our social networks develop powerful, mutually beneficial relationships. Social networks can drive planning and sales and increase industry presence. Is there power in social networking? You bet! And the power is within—it's in *you*.

8

PROLIFERATION IN NETWORKING

In the entrepreneur's development cycle, the stage at which proliferation in networking is viable is often the stage where the entrepreneur's head begins to feel like it might explode. There is so much to learn and so much to do in becoming a successful entrepreneur and growing a healthy business. This stage can become a make-or-break moment for entrepreneurs. It can shake one's confidence and make one yearn for simpler days when there wasn't so much pressure, so much riding on every decision. Some entrepreneurs actually get to the point where they feel like pulling out their hair. "What have I done?" she or he wails in a moment of sheer panic.

Well, guess what? It's natural to feel this way! In fact, almost every entrepreneur does at one time or another; most get to this point many times in a long business journey. It's natural to feel fear, even panic. The key is to not let yourself fall off the cliff. So much can be learned by creeping right up to the edge and staring into the abyss. Feel the fear, but look—really *look*! The longer you stand there, the more the fear will recede, and as it does, you will begin to see and make sense of a slew of opportunities that you just didn't see clearly before. One of those huge opportunities is called proliferation in networking, and it can push your business forward into uncharted waters where you'll discover more profit and more chances to expand and excel. Isn't this where every entrepreneur wants to go? I know I do! Proliferation in networking usually appears to entrepreneurs as a great opportunity to expand a customer base and sell more product, or as a frightening development that threatens to exhaust staff and erode the success you've achieved so far. Actually, proliferation in networking can be either, or both. How is this insight helpful? Knowledge is always helpful, regardless of its content. Let's look closely at this wonderful, scary gateway to opportunity.

Proliferation in networking refers first to the gathering and management of ever-expanding reams of information. Thanks to our global online social networking culture, we have immediate access to reams of information it would have taken years to tap into in the old days. Not only can we access this information instantly, we can swiftly organize it so that it is manageable, not overwhelming. We can pick and choose, be selective, and hone in on the information and details we need most, and we can do this with much greater speed and efficiency than our peers of just a couple of decades ago. Information is knowledge, and knowledge is power.

Proliferation in networking is also the greatest opportunity an entrepreneur has to listen to customers and learn what they really think. This deeper interaction with diverse customers will lead to improved customer service, product development, marketing, and quality assurance, among other benefits. The smart entrepreneur wants her business to improve its performance while providing an ever more pleasing experience for customers. As one earnest entrepreneur put it, "A business leader who is afraid of proliferation in networking is a cave dweller who has no idea what it really means to put his customers first. Soon, he'll be out of business."

Let's step back for a moment and ask an important question: *What does "proliferation" mean?* The word is a noun, and it means growth by the rapid multiplication of parts. In our world, "proliferation" has most often been used to describe the hell-bent-for-leather growth of deadly weapons. We actually appropriated the word from the French, where it was scientifically used to describe the formation or development of cells. The word's Latin roots include *proles*, which means "offsprings" or "descendants," and *fer*, which means "to bear" or "carry"; it can also mean "to bear children." Does this help to understand what the word proliferation means in the context of social marketing?

Let's approach it from the angle of branding. If a company creates and markets new products that are variations of the same product, this is a kind of brand proliferation. There doesn't have to be a deep plan or strategy behind this type of brand proliferation. Toothpaste is a great example. Check out various tubes next time you're at the store. Look at the buzzwords used for the various choices: fights gum disease, tarter control, whitening agent, breath freshener, strengthens enamel, organic tooth care. Doesn't it give you the sense that it could go on and on? Remember Bubba's classic soliloquy about shrimp in the movie *Forrest Gump*: "You can barbecue it, boil it, broil it, bake it, saute it. Dey's uh, shrimp-kabobs, shrimp creole, shrimp gumbo. Pan fried, deep fried, stir-fried. There's pineapple shrimp, lemon shrimp, coconut shrimp, pepper shrimp, shrimp soup, shrimp stew, shrimp salad, shrimp and potatoes, shrimp burger, shrimp sandwich." What is this but a brilliant recitation of proliferation of a brand?

Another example of brand proliferation I admire is the job that Nancy Bailey & Associates accomplished with Mr. Clean. Everyone knows Mr. Clean, right, the iconic all-purpose cleaner? He's in late middle age now, but he's still the virile, bald sailor in T-shirt and white trousers who never met a kitchen grease mess he couldn't defeat. Mr. Clean's creator Procter & Gamble decided some years ago to extend the brand to include products such as Magic Erasers (my favorite!), latex gloves, mops, scrubbers, and other cleaning accessories. Has this targeted brand proliferation worked?

With Mr. Clean–related sales exceeding $500 million a year since 2000, I would say so!

It's been said that when you see a logo, and a complete lifestyle immediately comes to mind, you want it. It's also true that brand proliferation has been and continues to be successful. An easy example is the luxury car market. Jaguar: sleek, powerful, independent. Or Mercedes-Benz: class, quality, influence, wealth. An example involving a smaller successful company is Bio-Logic Aqua's brand Research Water Life Science, and its proliferation with products like Nature's Mist Face of the Water and Nature's Tears EyeMist.

Brand Proliferation Exercises

Be observant and make a list of ten to twenty products. What are the key words you associate with each product? Have the businesses behind these products done a good job in exercising the art of brand proliferation?

Now, think of your own products and services. Ask staffers to come up with some branding ideas that would enhance your product performance. You might meet some surprises here.

Of course, many attempts at brand proliferation fail. One of my favorite fails was actress Eva Longoria's SHe Steakhouse for Women, which opened in Las Vegas and closed almost immediately. What were the odds that a brand extension like this would succeed? Not good and very long! Another fun fail was Dr. Pepper Marinade with its slogan, "More than Mesquite." Really? Who cares? How about Zippo, the makers of the iconic lighter. Zippo for some bizarre reason tried a product called Zippo the Woman Perfume—applied from a dispenser that looked just like a lighter. Who thought of such a thing?

Nestlé did much better with its Girl Scout Cookie candy bar—a candy bar–sized thin mint. Or how about Orville Redenbacher's variations on popcorn? Sure, we'll bite! Then there's the Disney Baby store with its myriad offerings of colorful character clothes and costumes for tots and toddlers. Who can resist? Apparently, no one!

Brand proliferation is an art form of sophisticated social marketing that every successful entrepreneur will dive into at one point or another. If your company is growing and doing well, it's inevitable that you will embrace brand proliferation as a necessity to long-term health and performance.

A variation of brand proliferation is mixed branding. This strategy produces the same product but markets it to different segments of the populace, using different names. Think Lexus and Toyota. The latter in the United States is considered a budget-minded, value brand. Lexus, however, is made for (and marketed to) a more affluent customer segment. Another example is Elizabeth Arden. This brand is available at Wal-Mart as Skin Simple.

Mixed branding can take the shape of three variant strategies, too. An example of sub-branding is Gillette for Women, which became the popular Venus product—a brand all its own. Cobranding combines qualities of two products within a company's portfolio of brands, and store branding takes place within a particular store or chain. The Elizabeth Arden example above is an example of store branding *and* mixed branding.

Other examples of mixed branding you'll easily recognize include Nike and Apple, Starbucks and Cineworld, McDonalds and Monopoly, Redbull and GoPro, Marks and Spencer & BP, Apple and U2, Uber and Barclaycard. The list can go on and on.

Proliferation in marketing has exploded in recent years because of the growth of so many communication channels. Back in the day, it was an accepted truth that there were nine communication channels that were used by most companies. These included magazine ads, newspaper ads, press releases, radio ads, television ads (called "spots"), collateral (white papers), billboard ads, letters, and events. The tenth channel, online activity, was at that point used by only a few entrepreneurial gamblers. It's hard to believe, but back then very few customers could be reached via email, message boards, and so on.

Today, everything has changed, or should I say, exploded. A savvy marketer and entrepreneur today will understand at least something about the following twenty-five communication channels, especially the last fifteen on this list.

1. Newspaper ads
2. Magazine ads
3. Broadcast TV ads
4. Cable TV ads
5. Satellite TV ads
6. Radio ads
7. Satellite radio ads
8. Billboard ads
9. Events
10. Webinars
11. PR
12. Email
13. Internet banners
14. PPC / AdWords
15. Streaming video ads (on other people's content)
16. Viral video (original content)
17. SEO/SEM
18. Collateral and downloadable assets (white papers, eBooks)
19. Mobile internet (QR codes, mobile search, etc.)
20. Video games
21. Podcasts
22. Short message service (SMS)
23. Instant messaging (IM)

24.   Social media
25.   Blogs

Product proliferation inevitably means product variety. Just consider this simple chart demonstrating the proliferation of certain products from 1970 to 2012.

Wow! Do you see the leap thanks to the proliferation of available communication channels? Communication is power. Relationships equal power. It is so true in business and marketing.

Let's take a moment to review what we've learned so far. Product proliferation takes place when a business decides to market variations of the same product. Product size and product use can vary. Even different color schemes and combinations are used in the marketing strategy. The result for the company is much desired diversity. It also enables the business to capture a larger percentage of the market.

There can also be dangers to the process. Product proliferation is so powerful that it can actually be difficult to control. If too many new products are released into the market, financial resources can be wasted. Customers can become confused and turned off by the effort. Remember that in the category of customer demand, the rule is change. Customer preferences will always change; the successful entrepreneur and business anticipates and meets this demand for change with products that satisfy evolving desires. Or, at the very least, the successful entrepreneur and business will be able to adjust with impressive dexterity to meet the demands of customers. Customers' changing desires can lead to an increase in the production and marketing of more product variations.

Proliferation networking has become a necessity for any successful, savvy, and expanding entrepreneur. Like every other challenge one faces, it's best to prepare and plan thoroughly, consult mentors and social network coworkers, friends, and customers, then dive in with enthusiasm and abundant positive energy. Do this, and you will find an abundance of likeminded people ready and willing to communicate and collaborate with you. This is the joy of creating and nurturing a successful business.

While doing so, you will encounter yet another development in our rapidly evolving global business world: the expansion of global network consulting. Network researchers have forecast that the global network consulting market will grow almost 7 percent from 2017 to 2021.

We know that data is expanding at a record pace and will continue to do so. There is no end in sight to this expansion. This data is growing as a result of the internet, social media, and, increasingly, mobile devices. As volume, variety, and velocity (the three Vs) of data grow, businesses scramble to store, manage, and make use of it. This is the point at which executive entrepreneurs begin to spend more on network analytic services and their data analytic skills. One can think of these organizations and their people as very specific mentors. They focus on one field—data—and nothing else. They can be helpful as long as an entrepreneur and business can use what they find. Those who get lost in the data (easy to do!) will be in trouble.

A major innovation introduced by consulting services is the move from existing infrastructure to a cloud-based networking service. Cloud computing is efficient, user friendly, and here to stay. The cloud-based system has made it possible for businesses to lower their internet usage charges while at the same time increasing their bandwidth. For the foreseeable future, companies that stay in business will be working with these new consultants, mentors of global networking.

It occurs to me that mastering proliferation networking taps into the same pleasure centers of the brain as doing crossword puzzles. I am so sure of this that I encourage you to experience crossword puzzles and Sudoku if you haven't already done so. Many studies have already suggested that there are some terrific brain-health benefits for those who work crossword puzzles, Sudoku, and other word and math games. These activities appear to stave off the onset or worsening of dementia and Alzheimer's disease. I believe they may also sharpen the entrepreneur's powers in the area of proliferation networking.

These activities are fun for me, and so is proliferation networking. Isn't fun often overlooked in just about everything we do? Yet who would argue against the idea that fun is essential to living a healthy life? Having fun is just as essential to running a healthy, successful business. First, it keeps you, the entrepreneur, healthier than you would be without it. Fun does the same for your staff, your clients, and your customers, too. In fact, the more you can incorporate fun into your planning, campaigns, and processes, the more success you will have along the way—and you will enjoy it so much more, too. Remember this key truth: It doesn't all have to be up to you. No need to make fun a burden that weighs heavily on your shoulders and your shoulders alone. Involve your staff! Ask for their input. Believe me, they will come up with some great ideas for having fun while you work toward your mutual business goals. Believe this, too: If you all succeed in creating a happy, fun work environment, everyone will be healthier and more positive. Everybody will go out of their way to pick up and help colleagues and customers. You'll be amazed at first at how the level of successful collaboration and cooperation rises when everyone is having fun.

Of course, I'm not suggesting that everybody should be acting like they're being constantly struck by the silly stick. A successful business environment shouldn't be a laugh riot. As in all healthy endeavors, the work environment fun should be balanced and focused. And let's never forget, success in which everyone shares is the most fun of all!

You might recall our earlier example of the woman who guided the recovery of the toy company. She realized right away that her team members were not having fun, so she did everything she could think of to encourage them to let loose. She designed the workspace so that it encouraged fun, and she successfully got them to play as if they were children again. What better way to design successful toys than to do so from the unique, unfettered view of children?

Now, let's have some fun!

Exercises in Fun

Make a list of the things you and your staff do every week to generate fun, to enjoy yourselves. Is there one activity you stage? Are there three? Five? Invite your staff to make their own lists. Convene a team meeting and share your lists. What did you learn from this sharing? Are you all on the same page, or are you surprisingly all over the map? If you're all over the map, what suggestions can all of you make to pull yourselves together into a more coherent, fun unit?

Another fruitful activity is to ask colleagues to share stories about having fun in the workplace. It's better to do this in a meeting rather than in writing so that people are socially engaging with each other.

Organize a Play Date

Yes, that's right. Organize a play date. Whether it's a conventional golf or bowling day or something odd, make plans to get together with colleagues and *play*. Take off together on hot air balloons. Spend a spirited day at a paintball range. Take a hiking tour, or sequester yourselves in a large room and build things with a mountain of Legos. The specific activity is less important than the interactive play itself. Try not to talk shop! Focus on what you are doing and let your conversations be guided by that. You will be surprised at how much anxiety you'll shed with a real play date. You'll also probably discover, when you return to your work environment, that you'll feel a lot lighter and quicker. Your brain will feel snappier, too. Fun and play are healers. They heal us because they rejuvenate and refocus us. Many entrepreneurs and businesses go sideways and fall flat because they never discovered the restorative benefits and pleasures of fun and play. Do you worry that your business is rolling down that path, but you're not sure? That's easy! Invite an outsider in for a day or two to observe your operation. A set of fresh eyes on what you do, on your procedures and processes and relationships, will work wonders. If you doubt it, just try it once and you will doubt no more. Fun and play not only heal, they restore balance to you, to others, and to your business endeavors. Fun and play must always be part of a successful business's infrastructure.

9

SUMMARY

We have shared a dynamic journey up to this point, and it's appropriate that we gather to review where we've been and what we've learned, and reaffirm where we intend to go. Let's look backward and forward at the same time, which is possible for any attentive entrepreneur!

All of us awakening entrepreneurs begin with a dream. If we're lucky, that dream has become a burning desire by the time we wake up. So we dream some more. We look around, taking stock of our existing resources, measuring our chances. We talk to family, friends, and trusted confidants, and we begin to plan. As the plans take shape, our excitement grows. We do our best to get all our ducks lined up in a row. Will we work from home at first or take a leap and rent a small office? Will we work alone or with one or more trusted allies who are willing to buy into the dream? Is this the best way to announce ourselves? Is this the shrewdest way to launch our enterprise? These questions and a million more like them will flood the budding entrepreneur's brain in the months, weeks, and days leading up to launch time. And then, the day comes. It's terrifying and wonderfully exciting. The doors and windows open and we are off and running. Well, maybe we're off and staggering, just a little! But mostly we're running, and thrilled to be doing so.

In today's highly competitive environment of globalization and rapid changes in technology, companies have to become adept at a number of activities in order not only to remain alive, but to acquire a consistent competitive advantage. To do this, companies have to anticipate a customer's needs and demands and learn to take confident risks by allocating sources for the fulfillment of those needs and demands. Successful companies also need to develop innovations by offering creative solutions. Companies must take a competitive approach in order to sustain their potent performance in the marketplace against all rivals, and accordingly, companies must be open-minded, innovative, and entrepreneurial in everything they do. In the process of pursuing innovation, companies must develop social capital containing certain elements. These elements include social networks, trust, norms, and common language and stories embedded in all relations between individuals and institutions. This constitutes and creates the additional sharing of information and opens doors to limitless opportunities.

Along the way, we're engaging in a process of constant entrepreneurial orientation. This orientation leads to the creation of new initiatives, practices, methods, and decision-making. The dimensions of entrepreneurial orientation include autonomy, risk taking, proactivity, innovation, and competitive aggressiveness.

To understand oneself in full entrepreneurial mode, one must take into account one's personal value system as well as the system of social values to which one belongs. One must also consider financial support and potential partners. Not taking these into account is bad planning, and we have seen how that always ends in disappointment, even disaster. A budding entrepreneur must develop the quality of perceived control. Putting into play the theory of planned behavior based on the theory of reasoned action, the entrepreneur must demonstrate perceived control over behavior and behavioral outcomes. Another way of saying this is that it's not just what you know, but how well you showcase what you know so that others can perceive it in positive and nonthreatening ways. Clarity is also essential. If you are confusing in your showcasing, then you stand little chance of succeeding in business—or in anything else, for that matter!

Understanding and predicting intention has always fascinated business and social network observers and fueled the efforts of entrepreneurs. Intention has been shown in many studies to be the best predictor of behavior, especially in those situations where the observation of behavior is difficult or involves unpredictable time lags. The creation of new entrepreneurial ventures is a good example of such behavior. Starting a business venture is not merely the result of coincidence; it falls into the category of planned behavior.

What is planned behavior? The theory of planned behavior is made up of these three predictors of intention: the attitude toward the behavior, the subjective norm, and the perceived behavioral control (indirect predictors of behavior). Attitude toward the behavior refers to the attractiveness of the behavior. In the context of entrepreneurial intention (i.e., a decision to start a business), the attitude is based on the degree of personal evaluation of the entrepreneurial profession and whether it is positively or negatively formulated.

"Subjective norm" refers to the perception of social pressure to perform an entrepreneurial behavior, such as launching an entrepreneurial venture. Somewhat surprisingly, in studies of entrepreneurial intention, social norms proved to be a weaker predictor of behavioral intention, between the strong ties, which develop between family members, friends, and ethnic groups, and the weak ties, which represent one's contacts with networks and organizations outside of a close and familiar community. Entrepreneurship is not only an economic phenomenon, it is also a social phenomenon that encompasses the social aspect of entrepreneurship. It's an interesting side note, for those of you who love reading, that entrepreneurship often appears in literature, mostly in the form of topics that explore and exploit social capital and social networking. There are also three common aspects that define social capital: social actors, resources, and relationships among actors. No matter where you begin your journey as an entrepreneur, you will come to the point, pretty quickly, where you will be acting in the realm of these three defining aspects of business life.

As our business plans take shape, we begin to pay closer attention to ROI—return on investment. We've learned that ROI depends on creating an atmosphere of trust and healthy collaboration. Do you remember that great saying we met back in Chapter Two? No company can be loved by its customers unless the employees love it first.

We know now that ROI depends on alignment, the lining up of personal and professional objectives. Without this alignment, ROI will falter. We also discovered that there are many intangibles regarding ROI; it's not just about a cash return on investment. There are intangible returns, too, such as growing contact lists. Attention to ROI also deepens relationships with customers, and it is an attractive feature when courting investors and other partners. ROI studies provide flexible opportunities for greater success and growth. That's a game that all entrepreneurs can warm up to.

We talked about the importance of follow-through and how a successful entrepreneur will always be persistent.

There are so many ways to be persistent. One can call someone at the same time every day, every other day, once a week, once a month. One can send an email following the same schedule. One can even go old-school and send letters on a prearranged schedule to customers, potential customers, stakeholders, and collaborators. One can arrange in-person meetings, scheduling breakfast, lunch, or coffee or tea every week or so. Being successfully persistent really means being appropriate and consistent.

That word—appropriate—is so important. It's so easy to be inappropriate. When an entrepreneur acts in an inappropriate way, all bets are off. No amount of persistence will save the entrepreneur who acts inappropriately. So, what is it to act in an inappropriate way?

Being pushy is a form of inappropriate behavior, and nothing is worse than this. Being pushy is terrible for business. It's bully behavior, whether or not it's intentional. Pushiness is usually the result of poor listening and a lack of empathy. If you do not listen well, you will not hear what the other person is trying to communicate to you. If for whatever reason you lack empathy, that means you can't feel what another person is feeling. The poet Theodore Roethke once wrote, "We think by feeling. What is there to know?" Isn't that a great reminder? You might want to copy it and put it on your desk somewhere for inspiration. We can't just think persistence; we need *to feel* persistence.

We've also examined potential in beneficial relationships. In a way, this point seems obvious, but there is more subtlety to it. If we create relationships that are beneficial to all parties, potential opportunities will arise from them. It's like how in gardening you want to put complementary plants side by side, ensuring that all will grow to their full potential. The potentiality in your beneficial relationships is limited only by your imagination. Beneficial relationships managed well result in positive gain: positive gain personally and positive gain professionally.

We discovered that nurturing beneficial relationships really does take conscious and constant work. They don't just happen. Within the workplace, it's wise to schedule sensitivity, tolerance, and diversity training and teach mediation skills. Some businesses even conduct brief meditation sessions at the beginning of the workday. It's amazing how even five minutes of meditation practice at the start of the day improves outlook and focus. Workers today need to be schooled in gender enlightenment, and all of this ought to happen with a spirit of excitement and discovery. Happy workers create a more successful business. Happy workers are snappy workers! I could walk through your place of business and tell you how well—or poorly—it's running just by taking note of the smiles I see and the laughter I hear as I walk through.

Talking and communicating are keys to success, and you should never stop sharpening those skills. A silent shop is a sullen shop, and a sullen shop is going nowhere you want it to go.

Curiosity is also a key to success. Doesn't one want to be fluid and learn from the experiences of older companies, strategic partners, and suppliers? I don't think I've ever heard anyone answer no to this question!

The point is, unless you can read minds and see the future, you really have no idea where a relationship may go when it begins. You can't get too caught up in trying to imagine what the other person is thinking, or what their motivations may be. All you can do is look to your own core values, your moral base, and make sure that they are appropriate for the given situation. All you can do is take care of yourself, be clear about your motives, be open, even vulnerable, and make space for the other person's openness and vulnerability. When relationships proceed on this foundation, they usually flourish, bringing benefits to both parties and extended connected parties. It's pure delight!

Anne Frank wrote, "Everyone has inside of him a piece of good news. The good news is that you don't know how great you can be! How much you can love! What you can accomplish! And what your potential is!" If

Anne Frank, in the face of the greatest imaginable fear and adversity, could

believe and write such words, can't we, too?

Then there is former president Barack Obama: "Focusing your life

solely on making a buck shows a certain poverty of ambition. It asks too

little of yourself. Because it's only when you hitch your wagon to something

larger than yourself that you realize your true potential."

Potential by its very nature is limitless, just as you are limitless. There is

no ceiling to what you can accomplish in your life and business. If there *are*

limits, they are limits that you have constructed. No one else is really

responsible for holding you back, because you are too powerful for that. If

you believe otherwise, then you have only tricked yourself into believing it.

Embrace the potential of beneficial relationships and you will not be

disappointed.

The practice of social networking focused us more on the nitty-

gritty of daily business practices. Remember Susan C. Young's "Mix,

Mingle, Glow"? The practice of networking is about creating opportunities

for others to shine, to stand out. If we practice networking while thinking

only of ourselves and the benefits that we will accrue, then we are flying nearly blind. Successful entrepreneurs learn to fly beyond the bars of their

ego cages to meet others in an environment that offers beneficial outcomes

for all. Trust and a willingness to share form the essential foundation for

successful social networking.

Entrepreneurs also need to remember that social networking

begins at "home," which is the workplace. Relationships between colleagues

today rely more than ever on mutual sharing and exchange via social

networks. Even in the same office, colleagues spend more time

communicating with each other via social networks than actually talking in

person. Workers gather around the water cooler a lot less these days. That's

why it makes sense to coordinate social network activities as part of the

daily office routine. By encouraging management and staff to comfortably

relate to each other via social networking, workers develop cooperation and

collaboration skills that might otherwise never be tapped. A lack of such

skills can prove a serious blow to any business's chances at success.

We also learned about three tried and true types of social

networking: operational social networking, personal social networking, and

strategic social networking. Do you remember the distinctions between

these types of social networking? Let's review.

Operational social networking is mostly internal. Operational social

networking is quick. What has to be done right now? The entrepreneur and the business rely heavily on in-house colleagues and staff to maintain and execute the procedures that are leading the business where it needs and wants to go. Remember the goal? A depth of understanding; the creation of relationships that are strong and enduring. At the same time, this is the method of social networking that is comfortable for most entrepreneurs, especially in the early stages of business. There is also a strategic danger. When entrepreneurs rely too much on internal players, they can miss opportunities to engage, learn from, and cooperate with potential players outside their businesses.

Personal social networking is a two-headed tactic through which one seeks to strengthen personal development and professional development. In personal social networking, entrepreneurs spend a lot of time referring others to new contacts, research, and useful information. Most of the contacts that entrepreneurs work with in personal social networking are external, which is directly opposite to most of the contacts entrepreneurs engage in with operational social networking. Personal social networking has a built-in higher degree of uncertainty than operational social networking because it's less clear who is appropriate for this or that task. In personal social networking, the entrepreneur wants to meet more and more contacts who can offer new referrals.

Finally, there is the social networking that focuses on future priorities and challenges that have not yet materialized—strategic social networking. Strategic social networking combines the strengths of operational and personal social networking. Entrepreneurs appeal more to stakeholders in this type of social networking. There is a greater balance of internal and external contacts; there is also a greater focus on the future. Strategic social networking depends on creating leverage, or outside-inside links.

Networking is also power in marketing. We've learned that what entrepreneurs are actually marketing is themselves and what makes them different. They're also marketing what they stand for.

To do so, entrepreneurs must come to terms with power. Power can corrupt and power can liberate. Power can be frightening. The power that resides within the entrepreneur herself can sometimes be the most terrifying power of all. For many reasons, people are often taught to hide or suppress their power. Keeping personal power under wraps is a way, we're often taught, to sidestep controversy and conflict. Some thrive on conflict and cutthroat competition, but many more do not and would prefer to finish back in the pack rather than act unscrupulously to get ahead. Getting comfortable with one's own power is a huge step, and a necessary step for the evolving entrepreneur. Remember the story I shared about the shy woman who started a publishing company? She persevered, doing extra background work before meeting with potential client and collaborators. That work paid off, boosting her confidence and allowing her gradually to succeed. Along the way, she became more comfortable reaching out and being contacted.

Power in networking requires a high degree of mindfulness. Abuse of power can damage a business and an entrepreneur's reputation, sometimes permanently. The best an entrepreneur can do is to develop the fluidity and flexibility that comes with an open mind. There is no substitute, in private life or in business, for being empathetic, open, and aware. The entrepreneur who can master this approach will thrive and prove time and again to be resilient.

Finally, let's briefly review proliferation in social marketing. Here is an earlier sentence that encapsulates the process: "Proliferation in networking refers first to the gathering and management of ever-expanding reams of information."

We learned that by the time entrepreneurs get to the point where they're ready for proliferation in marketing and branding, some of them are feeling like their heads will explode from the pressure. It all seems to happen so fast! The arc from waking up with a dream to diving into proliferation marketing can be mind-bending. Yet, if you remain grounded (meditation exercises help here), you can make the necessary adjustments. It's all about being fluid and relaxed while maintaining focus. Proliferation marketing has exploded in recent years because of the growth of so many communication channels. Also, the global social networks greatly speed up the process of gathering and sorting information, and this in turn leads to more opportunities for brand proliferation.

Proliferation networking is just that: opening more and more doors and windows to opportunity. Proliferation networking gives entrepreneurs even greater opportunities to listen to customers and potential customers and to craft promising product responses. Isn't this a grand goal? Proliferation networking is another terrific step along the successful entrepreneur's journey. What proliferation networking requires, you no doubt already possess. Otherwise, you wouldn't be in a position to even consider engaging in it!

So, here we are! You've become a Leaper! As a **LEAP SEVEN** partner, you've embraced your own personal adventure in **Launching Entrepreneurial Avenues of Possibilities**.

In the groundbreaking film *Black Panther*, T'Challa, king of the

African nation of Wakanda, issues a call-to-action, enlisting the talented and

resourceful to bring change to underprivileged communities around the

world. The film's memorable climax not only provides a rich and rewarding

call-to-action; it lays out examples of how the work can be done. We at

LEAP SEVEN are committed to this call-to-action, and we will contribute

a portion of the profits from the sale of this book to help build

entrepreneurs and businesses in underserved communities everywhere. This

great movie about culture, family, ethical decision-making, perseverance,

leadership, and humanity issues a challenge, which LEAP SEVEN Leapers

will accept. We will engage, using our talents and resources to change the

world by educating people. We will set good examples, provide coaching,

knowledge, contacts, and resources to help others, especially those without

many resources, to build and launch businesses in communities all over the

world.

Like me, you've awakened to the realization that you are a born

leader. Your dreams are meant not only to reward you, but to provide

beneficial opportunities and experiences for countless stakeholders,

customers, colleagues, and collaborators. The journey you are on will

benefit you and your family for years to come. You possess the tools and

the confidence you need to engage others, plan effectively, and create the future you have always desired.

You are your best asset, now and always, and others will buy into your energy, your planning, your promise, and your empathy. You are a **LEAP SEVEN** prototype. Embrace success! It is yours for the leaping!

10

INVITING ASPIRING ENTREPRENEURS & FUTURE LEADERS TO JOIN LEAP SEVEN

The 21st century world is driven by technology and the future truly belongs to entrepreneurs and business leaders of the digital world. However, most future leaders fail to find proper guidance and motivation while finding the way forward in their professional struggle. Leadership is all about translating vision into reality and Leap Seven is contributing in this area by empowering the entrepreneurs of the future and creating a collaborative community of intentional networks invested in the professional growth of members.

In this regard, based on the research Leap Seven and this text have developed learning development tools and resources to help entrepreneurs launch entrepreneurial avenues of possibilities. Dr. Marilyn Carroll, who is a college professor, a mother and a recognized American business leader has candidly written this guidebook, course material and setting up an organization geared towards coaching and mentoring new entrepreneurs.

The organization will also contribute a portion of the profits from the sale of this book to help build entrepreneurs and businesses in underserved communities everywhere. The modern entrepreneurial world is rapidly evolving, and this book has filled in the need of having an up-to-the-minute guide and roadmap can shorten the learning curve and speed up the process of achieving success.

Leapseven.org goal is to be a game changing organization which is all about translating dreams into real-life experiences because the ability of a good leader is to translate vision into reality. Leapseven.org is about several challenging areas of concerns for many entrepreneurs and address many key issues faced by the entrepreneurial community not only in the United States but also around the world as entrepreneurship knows no borders.

LEAP SEVEN Mission:

To create a collaborative community of intentional networks invested in the professional growth of members.

LEAP SEVEN Values:

Members act as allies who are innovative and spur change for the communities in which LEAP SEVEN members live and work. Why? We believe in cohesion, and that strength in members leads to openness and sharing to create something new that complements and helps all.

LEAP SEVEN Goals:

Our goals are to facilitate growth in relationships; foster intentional network expansion; inspire collaboration with diverse professional allies who invest in each other's professional growth; challenge traditional practices and build innovative solutions for the future.

Our primary goal with this inspiring book and in establishing Leapseven.org is simply to enable future leaders and aspiring entrepreneurs become successful in the competing industry and you can find out more about us on our website: www.LeapSeven.org

HOW CAN YOU HELP?

Join Leap Seven and invite seven of people to your network of intentional network. This is a network that will help you move to next level of possibilities. They help you to LEAP.

•

ABOUT THE AUTHOR

Marilyn Carroll is a Serial Entrepreneur and Founder of Carroll Beck, LLC. She is a business enthusiast and consultant renowned for establishing several start-ups and assisting businesses to derive optimal solutions that leverage competitive advantage.

Marilyn is a highly talented and accomplished professional, with outstanding success in implementing best practice methodologies and continuous improvement programs for functional management responsibilities. Over the years, she has gained solid backgrounds in organizational development, operations management, business analysis, research methodologies, mentorship, and coaching. She has also leveraged her Leadership and Management experience in working with talents from various backgrounds and professions including Accounting, Banking, Finance, Legal and Higher Education. Marilyn's major strength is her unique ability to blend academic, strategic and tactical expertise in changing unproductive 'at risk' operational practices to spawn results. Through creativity and dogged determination, she has successfully founded and operated several businesses that have grown to the zenith of their various industries.

She has authored different books and published several research works including Disruptive Leadership and Culture; Building Winning Strategies amongst many others. Marilyn is also a College Professor, affiliated with several professional organizations; and holds a Bachelor of Arts in Accounting, Bachelor of Science in Management, Master of Business Administration in Management and Global Leadership and Doctor of Philosophy in Organization and Management / Specialty Leadership.